JAMES MARTIN'S
ISLANDS to HIGHLANDS

Hardie Grant

QUADRILLE

Photography by Peter Cassidy

Contents

Foreword

As one of the leading lights and biggest supporters of the British food scene, James Martin shows everybody yet again how fantastic the food in Great Britain is. James never shies away from presenting Britain at its best, travelling to all corners in search of the finest produce, with the added bonus of meeting incredible chefs along the way and allowing them to showcase the great depth of culinary skill that we have in the UK.

This wonderful, beautiful book features some amazing recipes, ranging from simple through to simply stunning. It is a celebration of food that is now recognised the world over, and so much of that recognition is down to James and his talent for sniffing out people, places, ingredients and chefs.

As we all know, James is a proud Yorkshireman and has had a love of food since childhood. He comes from a farming background and the fact that he spent so much time getting dirt under his fingernails and toiling the land means he is completely in touch with the journey of ingredients, from their beginnings all the way through to the final cooking process. This is where James excels, and both his ability and his understanding of world cuisine are exceptional. He uses that talent to cook great dishes using outstanding British produce, which shows off not only James, the chefs and the food in a great light but also the produce of Great Britain.

This book is a fantastic representation of everything we should be proud of in this country. I can't think of a better person to be shouting about how great we are on these isles than James Martin. A wonderful Yorkshireman, a true friend of mine and the British food scene, and a force of nature telling everyone how it is with clear, crisp, easy-to-use recipes that you will want to cook again and again.

TOM KERRIDGE

PREVIOUS PAGES: SHETLAND
OPPOSITE: WALES

Introduction

Here we are again, on a great follow-up trip to the Great British Adventure but this time going further, higher and deeper into the world of British food and the people who make it. I've always said that the only way to fully understand and appreciate food is to see it being made, grown and produced and only then can you understand how much time and work it takes for the people involved.

We live in a world of convenience where food and drink are only a short visit or click away. It is so sad to see more and more food purveyors, from butchers and fishmongers to market-stall holders, becoming visitors' attractions rather than everyday necessities to community life. Food itself is increasingly mass-produced, tasteless and criminally cheap.

Having been on this amazing journey – and it truly was eye-opening – I have learnt so much from the passionate people who work in the hills, on remote islands and out at sea who make the beautiful food we can enjoy. There are so many highlights to tell you about, from the very first day I landed in the Isles of Scilly, a place so stunning that the beaches are as white as the Caribbean and where I swam with wild seals just 24 hours after landing; the Channel Islands where Mark Jordan and I rode on monkey bikes tasting the best potatoes and seafood platters in small bistros like Le Petit Bistro in Guernsey; Poole and its unbelievable millionaires' houses facing the second-biggest natural harbour in the world and its bass, clams, pork and cheese; Oxfordshire where Raymond Blanc opened his amazing hotel to the crew and me and showed me his new apple orchard; the Isle of Man and the TT with legend and good friend John McGuinness; over the water to Northern Ireland and the wonderful kelp from Rathlin Island and some of the best wasabi in the world produced in a kid's back garden; the breathtaking Welsh valleys and coastline and rallying through the forest; the east coast with its stunning array of castles leading up to the Holy Island of Lindisfarne and the mead once made by monks; the islands a stone's throw from Newcastle which are home to one of the best collections of puffins, seabirds and seals anywhere; Scotland – wow, Scotland – you have so much to give, where the Highland cows stood majestically on a hillside as I wandered among them to feed them; the Isle of Skye where I walked up a glen and saw a herd of deer at the top staring back at me; and in the end, a fitting tribute in Shetland – what scenery, what wildlife – where we spotted seals, dolphins, whales and birds of prey within 20 minutes of getting in a boat.

That last tribute was the icing on the cake for me, a cake of the whole of Great Britain in which every ingredient is special. If we don't support it and understand it, it will crumble. We all have the power to keep it special. I urge you to get out and explore it, taste our produce, stay over and eat the food these unique places serve and, most of all, open your eyes and look at how beautiful this place is that we call home.

JAMES

LIGHT
BITES

BBQ oysters and bacon with a pickled onion salad

SERVES 2

50ml olive oil
4 slices of white bread, diced
12 slices of streaky bacon, chopped
1 tablespoon Dijon mustard
2 tablespoons pickled onion vinegar
sea salt and freshly ground
  black pepper
120g bag mixed salad leaves
1 red little gem lettuce, sliced
small bunch of tarragon,
  leaves only
5 pickled onions, sliced
12 freshly shucked oysters
  in their shells

Mark Jordan's restaurant on the beach in Jersey tells you everything you need to know about the produce on this incredible island. The tidal stream and weather make this a special place for everything on- and off-land. Even the island itself doubles in size when the tide goes out – yes, doubles! We cooked this dish just outside Mark's place, called At the Beach.

Light your BBQ. When the coals are silvery in colour, it's ready to cook on.

Heat a non-stick flameproof frying pan on the BBQ. When hot, pour in half of the oil, add the bread and fry until golden and crisp, tossing a few times so the croutons cook evenly. Transfer to a bowl.

Drizzle the remaining oil into the same pan, then add the bacon and fry until crisp. Drain the fat into a separate large mixing bowl, and transfer the bacon to the bowl with the croutons.

Whisk the mustard and pickled onion vinegar into the bacon fat and season well. Add the salad leaves, lettuce, tarragon and sliced pickled onions to the bowl, toss well, then add half of the crispy bacon and croutons and toss again until everything is well dressed.

Put the oysters in their shells directly onto the coals of the BBQ and cook for 2–3 minutes. Use protective gloves or tongs to remove the cooked oysters from the BBQ, as the shells will be very hot.

To serve, lay the oysters around the outside of a large round plate, top with the remaining bacon and croutons and pile the dressed salad in the middle.

Crab beignets with lemon mayonnaise

SERVES 4

FOR THE MAYONNAISE
3 egg yolks
1 tablespoon Dijon mustard
200ml vegetable oil
pinch of sea salt
juice of 1 lemon

FOR THE BEIGNETS
85g salted butter, chopped
115g plain flour
2 eggs, beaten
100g white crab meat
50g brown crab meat
zest of 1 lemon, plus lemon
 halves for serving
sea salt and freshly ground
 black pepper
1–2 litres vegetable oil, for
 deep-frying, plus a little extra
 for greasing

This recipe uses a classic choux-pastry base, which is appropriate as Guernsey, where we cooked this, definitely has a French feel to it. The idea with the beignets is not to have the oil too hot, otherwise they become quite doughy in the centre. The great thing about them is that they work with veg like courgettes too.

Start by making the mayonnaise. Whisk the egg yolks and mustard together in a large bowl until smooth. Slowly pour in the vegetable oil, starting with a little drizzle and whisking well. This is easiest to do with an electric hand whisk. Continue to drizzle in the remaining oil, whisking all the time, until the mixture has thickened. Season with a little salt and lemon juice. Spoon into a bowl and set aside.

To make the beignets, put the butter into a medium saucepan and pour in 200ml water. Place the pan over a low-medium heat and cook until the butter melts, then bring to a rolling boil, add the flour and beat in with a wooden spoon. Take the pan off the heat and let the mixture cool slightly for a couple of minutes, then beat in the egg, a little at a time, until the mixture is soft and drops easily from the spoon. Fold in all the crab and the lemon zest and season with salt and pepper.

Heat the vegetable oil in a deep-fat fryer to 170°C/340°F or in a deep heavy-based saucepan until a breadcrumb sizzles and turns brown when dropped into it. (Note: hot oil can be dangerous; do not leave unattended.) Line a large plate with kitchen paper.

Dip a metal tablespoon in oil to grease it (this helps the mixture slide off easily), then scoop up 5 separate spoonfuls of the crab mixture and carefully drop them into the hot oil. Fry the beignets for 1–2 minutes until golden brown, then lift out with a slotted spoon to drain on the kitchen paper and sprinkle with salt. Repeat until you've used up all the mixture (it should make about 20 beignets).

Serve the hot crab beignets with the mayonnaise on the side and lemon halves for squeezing over.

Soused mackerel with beetroot salad

SERVES 4

2 mackerel, filleted and pin-boned
50ml gin
6 pink peppercorns
juice of 1 lemon
pinch of sea salt

FOR THE SALAD
3 tablespoons redcurrant jelly
50ml red wine vinegar
1 tablespoon Dijon mustard
sea salt and freshly ground
    black pepper
2 large cooked beetroot
    (not pickled in vinegar), diced

TO SERVE
1 pickled onion, thinly sliced
50g thick crème fraîche
small handful of micro herbs

This dish relies on the freshest mackerel and, in my opinion, it's one of the most underrated fish out there as well as one of the cheapest. We surprised all the cameramen when I went mackerel fishing and – within 30 seconds of dropping the line in – we pulled up nine! Simply prepared, this is a magical dish.

Put the mackerel on a board, flesh-side down, and use a sharp fish knife to cut through the skin in a criss-cross pattern.

Place the gin, peppercorns, lemon juice and salt in a shallow, non-metallic tray or dish and stir together. Lay the mackerel fillets on top, flesh-side down, and set aside for 30 minutes.

Meanwhile, heat the redcurrant jelly and vinegar together in a small pan to dissolve the jelly. Bring to the boil, then simmer until reduced by half. Put the mustard into a bowl, season, then pour the redcurrant sauce into it and whisk well. Add the diced beetroot and toss everything together.

To serve, divide the beetroot salad between 4 plates. Drain the mackerel from the marinade and place on top of the beetroot. Top each with sliced pickled onions, a quenelle of crème fraîche (see tip) and the micro herbs.

JAMES'S TIP
To make a quenelle, use two metal teaspoons: scoop up half the crème fraîche with one spoon, scrape the other spoon against the crème fraîche to lift it off the first spoon, then do the same again to make a smooth oval.

Dill blinis with Scottish smoked salmon and scrambled eggs

SERVES 4

FOR THE BLINIS

175g plain flour

1 teaspoon baking powder

2 eggs, separated

150ml full-fat milk

sea salt and freshly ground
  black pepper

small bunch of dill, chopped

25g salted butter

FOR THE SCRAMBLED EGGS

4 eggs

50ml double cream

25g salted butter

4 slices of smoked salmon,
  chopped

TO SERVE

8 slices of smoked salmon

100ml crème fraîche (optional)

1 lemon, cut into wedges (optional)

I cooked this dish in one of the most beautiful settings I have been in: Loch an Eilein (Loch of the Island). The stunning surroundings of forest and hills and the castle ruins that sit in the middle of the loch on a small island have recently been voted Britain's favourite picnic spot; it's no wonder. You need to go!

Heat a large flat griddle pan (or a heavy-based frying pan) over a medium heat until hot.

To make the blinis, put the flour into a large bowl, add the baking powder, egg yolks and milk. Season well and mix together.

In a separate clean and grease-free bowl, whisk the egg whites until stiff (you can use an electric hand whisk or balloon whisk for this), then fold into the batter along with the dill.

Dot the butter over the griddle pan. Once it is melted and foaming, spoon on the batter to form 8 discs. Cook for a couple of minutes until each one has puffed up and you can see bubbles appearing, then flip over and cook until golden on the other side. Lift onto a plate and set aside.

To make the scrambled eggs, whisk the eggs and cream together in a bowl. Heat the butter in a non-stick frying pan over a medium heat, then pour the egg mixture into the pan and cook gently, stirring occasionally, until just set. Stir through the chopped salmon and season with black pepper.

To serve, pile the slices of smoked salmon onto a serving plate with the blinis and serve the scrambled eggs alongside, with crème fraîche and lemon wedges on the side, if you like.

Scampi with lovage mayo

SERVES 2

FOR THE LOVAGE OIL
2 large bunches of lovage,
  stalks removed
200ml grapeseed oil

FOR THE MAYO
3 egg yolks
1 tablespoon Dijon mustard
1 teaspoon white wine vinegar
juice of 1 lemon

FOR THE SCAMPI
1–2 litres vegetable oil,
  for deep-frying
250g self-raising flour
350ml sparkling water
1 teaspoon sea salt
300g raw peeled langoustines
  or tiger prawns (about 12–14 tails,
  if bought in the shell)

TO SERVE
1 lemon, halved

True scampi should be made with langoustines, though there was a point when it was made with prawns or monkfish, due to the skyrocketing price of the langoustine. Sadly, like many ingredients from the UK, British langoustines are nearly all exported these days.

Lovage looks like celery leaves, but has a unique taste that can be used in soups, cordials and salads. When mixed with oil, it produces this amazing-coloured mayonnaise. Buy it at your local garden centre and grow it at home.

To make the lovage oil, bring a large saucepan of water to the boil. Fill a bowl with cold water and ice and set nearby. Blanch the lovage in the hot water for 10 seconds, then plunge into the bowl of iced water. Lift out and squeeze out any excess water, then place the lovage into a food processor along with the oil and blitz for 2 minutes.

Line a sieve with muslin and rest over a bowl. Tip the oil mixture into the muslin and strain – don't stir, just let all the oil slowly drip through.

Next, make the mayo. Whisk together the egg yolks and mustard in a bowl until smooth. Slowly drizzle in the lovage oil, whisking continuously. This is easiest to do with an electric hand whisk. Continue drizzling in the oil and whisking until the mixture has thickened, then whisk in the vinegar and lemon juice. Season to taste and set aside.

Heat the vegetable oil for the scampi in a deep-fat fryer to 180°C/350°F or in a deep heavy-based saucepan until a breadcrumb sizzles and turns brown when dropped into it. (Note: hot oil can be dangerous; do not leave unattended.) Line a large plate with kitchen paper.

Sift the flour into a large bowl, then pour in the water and add the salt, and mix together. Add the langoustines and toss to coat completely in the batter.

Use a large slotted spoon to lift the langoustines out of the batter and fry in batches until golden. Lift onto the kitchen paper to drain and season with salt.

Pile the scampi into a basket, spoon the mayo into a small bowl and serve with the lemon halves on the side for squeezing over.

Manx kipper soup with homemade bread

SERVES 4

600ml full-fat milk
3 Manx kippers
25g salted butter
1 shallot, finely diced
25g plain flour
25ml white wine
100ml double cream
200g cooked potato, diced
sea salt and freshly ground
  black pepper
small bunch of flat-leaf parsley,
  chopped

FOR THE BREAD

500g strong plain bread flour,
  plus extra for dusting
2 teaspoons table salt
7g sachet quick yeast
3 tablespoons olive oil

TO SERVE

small bunch of chives, chopped
extra double cream and olive oil,
  for drizzling

Moore's Smokehouse stayed open for me to have a look round when we finished filming in Peel. It's well worth the trip, as smoking fish here has a long history thanks to the abundance of spawning herring once caught in large volumes around the island but which are now also bought in fresh from further afield. Spawning fish aren't great to eat fresh; curing and smoking results in a far tastier product. You can buy these kippers online too. Eat grilled with butter, or make this soup.

Start by making the dough for the bread. Place all the ingredients into the bowl of a freestanding mixer, fitted with a dough hook. Pour in 300ml water and knead on a medium speed for 5 minutes until the dough is smooth and comes together in a ball. You can also do this by hand: mix everything together in a large bowl with the water, then knead lightly on a floured surface for 8–10 minutes until smooth.

Lightly dust a clean work surface and a baking sheet with flour. Shape the dough into a round, then place on the prepared baking sheet and leave to prove for 1–2 hours until doubled in size.

Meanwhile, preheat the oven to 200°C (180°C fan)/400°F/gas 6. Bake the proved dough for 30 minutes.

Pour the milk into a large, wide pan and add the kippers. Bring to the boil, then reduce the heat to low and poach the kippers for 3 minutes. Scoop the fish out onto a plate, reserving the poaching milk, and let cool a little. When cool enough to handle, flake the fish off the bones and set aside (discarding the head and bones).

Heat the butter in a large pan over a medium heat, add the shallot and fry for about 2 minutes until starting to soften. Stir in the flour and cook for 1 minute, then pour in the wine and bring to the boil. Whisk in the poaching milk and cream, then simmer over a low heat for a few minutes until warmed through, stirring continuously. Add the potatoes and flaked kippers to the pan, cover and cook for a further 2–3 minutes, then season well and add the parsley.

Use a ladle to divide the soup among 4 warm bowls. Sprinkle over the chives and drizzle with extra cream and a little extra olive oil, if you like. Serve with the homemade bread on the side.

NEWLYN, CORNWALL

Newlyn Harbour fried fish with chipotle dressing and deep-fried parsley

SERVES 6

100ml dry white wine

750g mussels, cleaned
  (see tip)

1–2 litres vegetable oil, for frying

200g semolina

100g plain flour

1 tablespoon cayenne pepper

sea salt and freshly ground
  black pepper

1 egg, beaten

8 small monkfish fillets
  (about 100g each)

4 megrim fillets, trimmed

FOR THE DRESSING

200ml crème fraîche

1 tablespoon chipotle paste

sea salt and freshly ground
  black pepper

TO SERVE

small bunch of flat-leaf parsley,
  thoroughly dried with
  kitchen paper

2 limes

This dish is as quick to cook as it was to eat it in the amazing setting of Newlyn Harbour, surrounded by fishing boats delivering their catch, and dodging the ever-increasing number of seagulls above our heads. Smoky chipotle paste is widely available these days and is ideal for making this punchy dressing.

Heat a large non-stick saucepan with a lid over a medium heat until hot, then pour in the wine. Add the mussels and immediately pop the lid on the pan and cook for 3–4 minutes. Strain the cooking liquor through a fine sieve and into a bowl. Cool the mussels a little, then pick the meat out of the shells and put in a bowl.

Meanwhile, heat the vegetable oil in a deep-fat fryer to 190°C/375°F or in a deep heavy-based saucepan until a breadcrumb sizzles and turns brown when dropped into it. (Note: hot oil can be dangerous; do not leave unattended.) Line 2 large plates with kitchen paper.

In a large shallow bowl, mix the semolina, plain flour and cayenne pepper and season well. Whisk the egg into the mussel liquor to combine, season and whisk again. Dip the mussels, monkfish and megrim into the egg mixture, then coat them in the semolina mixture.

Deep-fry the fish in batches, starting with the monkfish, and cook for 3 minutes. Next, do the megrim and cook for 2 minutes, and finally cook the mussels for 1 minute. Use a slotted spoon to lift each portion of fish onto the kitchen paper to drain and season with salt.

Meanwhile, whisk together the dressing ingredients in a bowl, season to taste, and set aside.

Finally, deep-fry the parsley for 30 seconds until crisp and remove with a slotted spoon to drain on the kitchen paper.

To serve, pile the fish onto a warm platter, drizzle the dressing over the top and scatter over the parsley. Use a fine grater to grate lime zest over the dressing, then cut the limes in half and serve alongside.

JAMES'S TIP

Fresh mussels need to be alive before you cook them. To prepare them, pull off the stringy beards, knock off any barnacles and give the shells a scrub in fresh water to clean. Throw away ones with broken shells or any that don't close tightly when you tap them.

Beachside surf and turf wraps

MAKES 3–4

500ml Greek yogurt
1 tablespoon baharat
1 teaspoon ras-el-hanout
1 teaspoon ground cumin
1 teaspoon ground coriander
5-cm piece fresh root ginger, grated
sea salt and freshly ground
  black pepper
450g sirloin steak, cut into
  4-cm cubes
6 scallops, cleaned, roes removed

FOR THE SALAD
½ red cabbage, thinly sliced
1 red chilli, sliced
50ml white wine vinegar
1 teaspoon sea salt
2-cm piece fresh root ginger, grated
a few sprigs of coriander, chopped
a few mint leaves, chopped

TO SERVE
3–4 soft white flatbread wraps
a few extra fresh coriander and
  mint sprigs

I put this steak and scallop combo in a wrap, as it's a practical way to eat them while down at the beach; you can use any meat or shellfish combination here. In Cornwall, the meat is as good as the fish, as the pasture is sublime. If you want to taste it as its best, try Paul Ainsworth's places: The Mariners and Paul Ainsworth at Number 6. They showcase top-class cooking using the best of Cornish produce.

Baharat and ras-el-hanout are easily bought in larger supermarkets or Middle Eastern grocers.

If using wooden skewers, place them to soak in a bowl of water for 20 minutes before cooking. Light your BBQ. When the coals are silvery in colour, it's ready to cook on.

To prepare the skewers, put 300ml of the Greek yogurt into a large bowl, then add the spices and grated ginger. Season and mix well. Add the chopped steak and scallops, toss to coat thoroughly, then thread the cubes of steak and scallops onto the skewers.

Place the skewers on the BBQ and cook for 3 minutes on one side, then turn and cook for a further 3 minutes on the other side, until the meat is well charred.

Meanwhile, make the salad. Mix all the ingredients in a bowl and set aside until the skewers are cooked.

To serve, spread each wrap with the remaining Greek yogurt. Remove the steak and scallops from the skewers and divide among the wraps, spoon some of the salad on top and scatter over the extra coriander and mint sprigs.

NEWLYN HARBOUR, CORNWALL

BBQ lamb baguette

SERVES 4–6

8 lamb sausages
2–3 tablespoons olive oil
1 bunch of spring onions, trimmed

FOR THE SAUCE
600g lamb mince
2 shallots, diced
1 garlic clove, sliced
1 green chilli, diced
200g soft dark brown sugar
100ml ketchup
50ml soy sauce
50ml white wine vinegar
2 tablespoons chipotle paste
small bunch of coriander, chopped
small bunch of mint, chopped

TO SERVE
1 large baguette
25g garlic butter,
  at room temperature
small bunch of coriander, chopped
small bunch of mint, chopped
2 tablespoons crispy fried
  onions (store-bought)

I made this using a combination of lamb sausages and lamb mince with crispy onions and it was one of the crew's favourites. Lamb sausages, as I found, can be quite tricky to cook perfectly on a BBQ, so you can do this in a pan if it's easier.

Light your BBQ. When the coals are silvery in colour, it's ready to cook on.

Heat a non-stick flameproof frying pan on the BBQ. When hot, add all the ingredients for the sauce and bring to the boil. Simmer for 10 minutes, stirring occasionally.

Drizzle the sausages with 1–2 tablespoons of the oil and pop onto the BBQ or into a separate non-stick frying pan over a medium-high heat. BBQ or fry for 10 minutes, turning every couple of minutes, until golden and cooked through.

Drizzle the spring onions with the remaining oil and cook on the BBQ alongside the sausages for a couple of minutes, turning occasionally, until charred.

To serve, split the baguette lengthways through the middle and spread with the garlic butter. Fill with the herbs and pile the sausages on top. Spoon over the sauce, top with the griddled spring onions, then sprinkle over the crispy fried onions. Slice into 4–6 pieces and let everyone dig in. Hand round paper napkins, too, as this is a saucy, messy feast.

Flatbread with spiced venison and chimichurri

SERVES 2

FOR THE FLATBREAD DOUGH

3g fast-action dried yeast

150ml warm water

325g strong plain bread flour,
  plus extra for dusting

pinch of sea salt

60ml natural yogurt

FOR THE SMOKED YOGURT

50g tea leaves (any type)

100g demerara sugar

90g rice (any type)

200ml Greek yogurt

FOR THE TOPPING

300g venison loin, sliced 1 cm thick

1 teaspoon mild chilli powder

1½ teaspoons garam masala

1 teaspoon ground cumin

1 teaspoon black onion seeds

50ml vegetable oil

sea salt and freshly ground
  black pepper

zest and juice of 1 lime,
  plus 1 lime, halved, to serve

100ml beef stock

a few micro coriander sprigs

FOR THE CHIMICHURRI

50ml red wine vinegar

2 garlic cloves, roughly chopped

1 green chilli, roughly chopped

1 shallot, roughly chopped

small bunch each of coriander and
  mint, leaves picked

100ml olive oil

Wine & Brine is a great restaurant in Moira, County Armagh. Chris McGowan is the brains in the kitchen and what a meal I had thanks to his brining and curing methods. This dish is inspired by one on the menu with lamb, made here with venison instead.

Start by making the dough for the flatbread. Pour the yeast into the warm water and stir to dissolve. Sift the flour into a large bowl and stir in the salt. Make a well in the middle, add the yogurt and then the yeasted water. Use a spoon to stir everything together to make a rough dough, then tip onto a clean work surface and knead for 5 minutes until smooth. The dough should be sticky. Shape into a ball, then place in a clean bowl and cover. Set aside to rise for about 2 hours.

Next, make the smoked yogurt. Wrap the tea, sugar and rice in a parcel of foil and use the tip of a sharp knife to cut a couple of holes in it. Lay flat in a heavy-based frying pan. Spoon the yogurt into a shallow dish, season, then put the dish into the frying pan, too. Cover the frying pan with foil and place over a medium heat. Cook for 5 minutes to smoke the yogurt, then remove from the heat and set aside.

Preheat the oven to 220°C (200°C fan)/425°F/gas 7 and slide a large rectangular baking sheet into the oven to heat up.

Put the venison into a bowl and add the chilli powder, garam masala, cumin, black onion seeds and vegetable oil. Season well with salt and pepper. Add the lime zest and juice, stir together, then set aside.

When the dough has risen, lightly dust a clean work surface with flour. Lift the dough onto the work surface and lightly knead it to knock it back. Roll it out to a rectangle of about 30 x 12cm. Carefully transfer the flatbread to the baking sheet. Bake for about 12 minutes.

Meanwhile, heat a large dry frying pan over a medium-high heat, add the marinated venison and fry for 2 minutes, then pour in the stock and cook for a further 3–4 minutes.

Put all the ingredients for the chimichurri (reserving a few mint leaves for garnish) into the bowl of a food processor and whiz until smooth.

Slide the flatbread onto a large board and top with the hot fried venison. Spoon the smoked yogurt over the top, then drizzle over the chimichurri. Squeeze over some lime juice, scatter with the micro coriander and the reserved mint leaves, then serve.

Beef carpaccio with candied walnuts, pears and a blue cheese dressing

SERVES 8

1kg beef fillet

25g salted butter

a few sprigs of thyme, leaves picked

sea salt and freshly ground black pepper

FOR THE CANDIED WALNUTS AND PICKLED PEARS

750g caster sugar

200g walnut halves

300ml vegetable oil, for frying

25ml white wine vinegar

2 Conference pears

FOR THE DRESSING

100ml mayonnaise

125g blue cheese (any type)

1 teaspoon Worcestershire sauce

TO SERVE

small handful of watercress and celery tops

extra virgin olive oil, for drizzling

In my opinion, beef carpaccio should always be done using fillet of beef. You can pan-fry it to get a nice colour outside but the best way is on a BBQ: get it flaming so it chars, then you get that great combination of raw meat interior and charred exterior.

Take the beef out of the fridge around 20 minutes before cooking to bring it up to room temperature.

Melt the butter in a large frying pan over a medium-high heat, then quickly sear the beef all over, turning as soon as each side is browned.

Tear off 2 sheets of clingfilm and place on top of each other. Sprinkle the thyme and plenty of salt and pepper all over the clingfilm, then pop the beef on top and roll the clingfilm tightly around it. Chill in the fridge for 1 hour.

To make the candied walnuts, pour the sugar into a large pan, add 75ml water and heat gently. As soon as the sugar has dissolved, stir the walnuts through the syrup. Lift out with a slotted spoon and into a bowl. Set the syrup aside – it'll be used to pickle the pears.

Heat the vegetable oil in a deep-fat fryer to 180°C/350°F or in a small deep heavy-based saucepan until a breadcrumb sizzles and turns brown when dropped into it. (Note: hot oil can be dangerous; do not leave unattended.) Line a large plate with kitchen paper.

Carefully lower the walnuts into the oil and deep-fry, in batches, for 1 minute. Lift out and drain on the kitchen paper.

Add the vinegar to the reserved sugar syrup, then use a potato peeler to peel strips from the pears and drop them into the syrup. Leave to pickle for 10 minutes, then lift out with a slotted spoon and set aside.

Combine the dressing ingredients in the bowl of a food processor and whiz until smooth. Season and whiz again to combine.

To serve, take the clingfilm off the beef, place on a board and use a sharp knife to slice it into thin rounds. Arrange the beef slices over a platter, lay a sheet of clingfilm on top and press down firmly to get the slices even thinner, then remove the clingfilm. Scatter over the walnuts, followed by the pear slices, sprigs of watercress and celery tops. Dot with the dressing and drizzle over a little olive oil, if you like.

Coarse terrine

SERVES 8

TO LINE THE TIN
16 thin slices of pork lardo

FOR THE FILLING
250g pork fillet, diced
150g bacon lardons
150g pork lardo, diced
250g pork belly, skin removed
  and diced
150g chicken livers, sinew and
  gland removed, diced
1 shallot, diced
small bunch of thyme,
  finely chopped
4 garlic cloves, crushed
1 teaspoon freshly grated nutmeg
1 heaped teaspoon ground mace
1 teaspoon ground cloves
1 tablespoon fennel seeds
2 eggs, beaten
50ml double cream
50ml brandy
sea salt and freshly ground
  black pepper

TO SERVE
8 slices of crusty bread
chutney of your choice

The old saying that happy pigs taste better is the perfect slogan for the Lake District – some of the greatest chefs in the world buy their pork from this area. It was a privilege to spend the day with the great Clare Smyth and discover just some of the people who supply her restaurant. This terrine is similar to the classic French style – rustic but full of flavour – and uses lardo (not to be confused with bacon) to add texture.

Preheat the oven to 160°C (140°C fan)/325°F/gas 3.

Line a 30-cm terrine mould, or a 2-lb loaf tin, with the lardo slices, slightly overlapping each piece and making sure the inside of the mould is completely covered. Leave the edges hanging over the outside.

Put all the ingredients for the filling into a large bowl, season well and mix everything together until well combined. Spoon the mixture into the lined mould, pressing down lightly and levelling the surface. Pull the excess lardo over the top to cover then place a piece of greaseproof paper on top. Cover with the terrine mould lid or with a piece of strong foil secured with string, then lift into a deep roasting tin and pour in enough water to come about 5cm up the side of the mould. Cook in the oven for 1 hour on the bottom shelf, until an inserted skewer meets no resistance.

Lift the mould out of the tin, remove the lid or foil and sit on a wire rack to cool.

Weight down the terrine (a couple of tin cans work well), then chill in the fridge overnight.

When you're ready to serve, remove the weight and greaseproof paper, carefully slide a butter knife around the edge to loosen the terrine and turn out onto a board. Slice and enjoy with the crusty bread and chutney.

Scone Palace cheese and ham toastie

SERVES 6–8

1 oblong sourdough loaf,
   about 30cm long
24 slices of thick-cut unsmoked
   ham (or 12 slices of ham plus
   200g pancetta, fried until crisp)
small bunch of flat-leaf parsley,
   chopped
100g whisky-soaked cheese
   (of your choice), crumbled

FOR THE SAUCE
25g salted butter
2 tablespoons plain flour
100ml full-fat milk
150ml double cream
300g Isle of Mull Cheddar, grated
freshly ground black pepper

TO SERVE
chutney of your choice

I cooked this dish in the grounds of Scone Palace, one of Scotland's most important stately homes. I didn't, however, use one of their beautiful towels for the last step of the recipe on the BBQ; I used one from a Travelodge – sorry! It's even better baked in the oven but, my god, this tastes as good as it looks.

Preheat the oven to 200°C (180°C fan)/400°F/gas 6. Alternatively, light your BBQ. When the coals are silvery in colour, it's ready to cook on.

To make the sauce, heat the butter in a saucepan (flameproof if BBQing) over a medium heat. Once the butter is melted and foaming, whisk in the flour. Cook for 1–2 minutes, then whisk in the milk, cream and two-thirds of the grated Cheddar. Cook until the mixture is bubbling, then remove from the heat and season with black pepper.

Using a sharp bread knife, cut the loaf of bread into at least 12 slices, each about 2cm wide, stopping within 1cm of the bottom of the loaf so the slices remain attached at the base. Take a piece of foil, large enough to wrap around the entire loaf, place a slightly smaller piece of baking parchment on top of it, and place the loaf on the baking parchment. Spoon some of the cheese sauce into each cavity, then fill each one with 2 slices of ham and a little chopped parsley. Spoon any remaining sauce over the top and scatter with the remaining Cheddar and the whisky cheese. Wrap up the parcel tightly, place on a baking sheet and bake for 20 minutes. Alternatively, pop it onto the BBQ, cover completely with a damp towel and BBQ for 20 minutes.

To serve, open the parcel, slice into portions and serve with chutney.

Welsh rarebit with bacon and cockles

SERVES 4

8 slices of unsmoked back bacon
50g salted butter
350g Caerphilly cheese, grated
150g Welsh cheddar, grated
1 tablespoon English mustard
1 teaspoon Worcestershire sauce
1 teaspoon Tabasco sauce
3 egg yolks
2 tablespoons plain flour
50ml full-fat milk
50ml bitter beer/pale ale
sea salt and freshly ground
   black pepper
200g shelled cockles

FOR THE CHUTNEY
100g demerara sugar
1 small shallot, diced
50ml white wine vinegar
50g golden sultanas
200g cherry tomatoes, halved
a few sprigs of tarragon

The key to a good Welsh rarebit is that combination of cheese, mustard, Tabasco and Worcestershire sauce, and the texture, which is why I think cooking it first works best. Whether on its own on toast, or served as I have here, it's a winner. It would be delicious with some crusty bread. For the filming, it was also a good excuse to get the new mobile pizza oven out for the first time.

Preheat the oven to 200°C (180°C fan)/400°F/gas 6.

Spread the bacon out in a large roasting tin, dot with the butter and roast for 10 minutes.

Meanwhile, heat a medium non-stick pan over a medium heat and add the cheeses, mustard, Worcestershire sauce and Tabasco sauce, stirring everything together until the cheese has melted and the mixture is well combined. Beat in the egg yolks and flour, then reduce the heat a little, pour in the milk and beer and season well. Cook gently, stirring, for a further 2 minutes.

Remove the roasting tin from the oven, spoon the cockles evenly over the bacon, then spoon the cheese sauce all over the top. Return to the oven to bake for 5 minutes until the top is golden and bubbling.

To make the chutney, heat the sugar in a medium heavy-based saucepan until the sugar has melted and turned a golden caramel colour. Add the remaining ingredients and bring to the boil, then reduce the heat and simmer for 5 minutes.

To serve, divide the rarebit among serving plates and spoon the chutney on the side.

Sharpham cheese board

SERVES 8

FOR THE BAKED SAVOUR
4 fresh vine leaves
200g Sharpham Savour cheese,
  cut into chunks
4 pickled onions, sliced
25ml Sauternes wine
100ml double cream
6 slices of streaky bacon

FOR THE BAKED CREMET
2 x 150-g Sharpham Cremet cheeses
2 garlic cloves, sliced
a few rosemary sprigs, roughly torn

FOR THE FRIED ELMHIRST
vegetable oil, for deep-frying
75g panko breadcrumbs
a few fresh thyme sprigs, chopped
2 eggs, beaten
50g plain flour
sea salt and freshly ground
  black pepper
4 fresh vine leaves (optional)
about 200g Sharpham Elmhirst
  cheese, sliced into 4 pieces

SERVING SUGGESTIONS
fresh vine leaves, to decorate
1 x 250-g Sharpham Garlic and
  Chives Rustic round, halved
handful of white or red grapes
a few sticks of celery with leaves
8 slices of toasted sourdough bread
8 pickled onions
selection of chutneys

The Sharpham Dairy started in 1981 and has since amassed a large range of award-winning handmade cheeses using their brilliant Jersey cow's milk. They also make goat's cheese and produce brilliant English wines to match their products. This idea takes cheese boards to another level. It would also work well with brie or camembert if you can't get hold of the Sharpham varieties, which are available in plenty of online delis.

Preheat the oven to 200°C (180°C fan)/400°F/gas 6.

For the baked Savour, use the vine leaves to line a deep ovenproof dish, measuring about 20 x 15 x 7cm. Scatter the cheese over the base, followed by the pickled onions. Pour over the wine and cream and top with the bacon. Bake on the top shelf of the oven for 15 minutes.

For the baked Cremet, slice the top off each cheese and pop them into an ovenproof ramekin, about 10cm round x 3cm deep. Stud the cheese with the sliced garlic and rosemary sprigs and bake on the middle shelf of the oven for 10 minutes.

For the fried Elmhirst, heat the vegetable oil in a deep-fat fryer to 170°C/340°F or in a deep heavy-based saucepan until a breadcrumb sizzles and turns brown when dropped into it. (Note: hot oil can be dangerous; do not leave unattended.) Line a plate with kitchen paper.

Mix the panko breadcrumbs and thyme together in a shallow dish. Put the egg in another separate shallow dish and the flour in another. Season the flour well. If using the vine leaves, wrap each piece of cheese in 1 leaf, then dip each piece first in the flour, then in the beaten egg, then the breadcrumb mixture to coat completely. Carefully lower into the hot oil and fry for around 1 minute until golden and crispy. Remove with a slotted spoon to drain on kitchen paper.

To serve, take a very large board and cover it with fresh vine leaves, if using. Position the Sharpham Garlic and Chive Rustic halves on top, followed by the baked Savour, fried Elmhirst and baked Cremet. Decorate with grapes, celery, the toasted bread and the pickled onions, if using. Spoon the chutneys into several small dishes and arrange in and amongst the ingredients. Let everyone dig in!

Violet artichokes with wild mushrooms and hollandaise

SERVES 4–6

12 baby violet/purple artichokes
juice of 1 lemon
3 garlic cloves, crushed
6 black peppercorns
a few sprigs of tarragon, plus
   a few extra for the mushrooms
2 tablespoons olive oil
25ml white wine

FOR THE WILD MUSHROOMS
300g wild mushrooms,
   brushed clean and torn if large
25g salted butter

FOR THE HOLLANDAISE
250g salted butter
4 tablespoons white wine vinegar
1 shallot, diced
6 white peppercorns
a few sprigs of tarragon
3 large egg yolks
sea salt and freshly ground
   black pepper

The Walnut Tree Inn in Wales is an icon of the Welsh food scene and has one of the greatest owners and chefs in the business. Shaun Hill is a legend and genius at the hobs and it was one of those pinch-yourself moments when I got to work alongside him in his kitchen.

To prepare the artichokes, trim each stalk to 6cm in length. Use a peeler to shave the tough outer layers of the stalk. Cut off the top third of the leaves, then cut each artichoke in half lengthways. Pop the halves into a large bowl of cold water and add the lemon juice.
   Bring a large pan of water to the boil and add the garlic, peppercorns, tarragon sprigs, olive oil and white wine. Add the artichokes, cover with a lid and bring to the boil, then reduce to a simmer and cook for 15 minutes. Drain well and set aside.
   To clarify the butter for the hollandaise, gently melt the butter in a saucepan over a low heat. As it melts you will see it split: the milk solids will collect in the base of the pan and a white foam will form on top. Skim off and discard the foam, then carefully pour the golden clarified butter into a separate bowl, leaving the milky liquid behind.
   Put the vinegar, shallot, peppercorns and tarragon sprigs into a small saucepan and bring to the boil, then simmer until reduced to about 2 tablespoons. This is called a 'gastric'.
   To make the hollandaise, rest a large bowl over a pan of simmering water, ensuring the base doesn't touch the water. Add the egg yolks to the bowl and strain in the gastric mixture. Whisk together to combine, then slowly add the melted clarified butter. Drizzle it in very slowly while whisking continuously until the mixture gradually thickens into a sauce. Season.
   Fry the mushrooms with the butter in a large frying pan for 2–3 minutes, until golden and softened. Season well, sprinkle over a few roughly torn tarragon leaves and stir together.
   Preheat the grill to high.
   Pile the artichokes into a large ovenproof dish. Scatter the fried mushrooms over the top, then drizzle over the hollandaise. Pop under the grill to cook for a couple of minutes until the sauce bubbles and turns golden. Serve immediately.

RATHLIN ISLAND, NORTHERN IRELAND

Kimchi with kelp and chargrilled courgettes

SERVES 8

1 tablespoon olive oil, plus extra
    for drizzling
2 large courgettes, each cut
    into 4 pieces lengthways

FOR THE KIMCHI
1 medium white cabbage, shredded
1 tablespoon sea salt
3 garlic cloves, crushed
10-cm piece fresh root ginger,
    grated
3 star anise
100g caster sugar
100ml rice wine vinegar
100ml white wine vinegar
small bunch each of mint and
    coriander, chopped
2 red chillies, chopped
zest and juice of 2 limes
1 teaspoon kelp seaweed,
    soaked and chopped

FOR THE MAYONNAISE
3 egg yolks
1 tablespoon Dijon mustard
200ml vegetable oil
small bunch of coriander
1 tablespoon kelp pesto (optional)
zest and juice of 1 lime

It was fantastic to see kelp being harvested off the coast of Rathlin Island in Northern Ireland. The old, derelict kelp house is one of the first things you see on the short ferry ride over to the island. Walk the short distance from the ferry to the guys at Islander Rathlin Kelp and you will see what brilliant work they are doing to keep the industry alive. I have been buying their kelp noodles online ever since visiting them and they taste amazing.

The day before you want to serve this, make the kimchi. Put the cabbage into a bowl with the salt and leave for 10 minutes to draw out any juices. Drain and rinse the cabbage.

Put the garlic, ginger and star anise into a piece of muslin and tie with string. Put the sugar and both types of vinegar into a small saucepan. Add the muslin bag to the pan and heat gently to dissolve the sugar. Bring to the boil and turn off the heat. Add the cabbage, toss everything together, then transfer to a bowl or ziplock bag and chill overnight.

To make the mayonnaise, put the egg yolks and mustard into the bowl of a mini food processor and whiz to combine. With the motor running, slowly drizzle in the oil, then add the coriander, kelp pesto (if using), lime zest and juice and whiz again. Spoon into a piping bag.

Take the star anise bag out of the kimchi and drain the liquid. Add the mint, coriander, chillies, lime zest and juice, and the kelp. Stir everything together.

Heat a griddle pan to smoking hot. Drizzle the olive oil over the courgette slices and char in batches for 2 minutes on each side. Chop into 2–3-cm wide pieces. Stir into the kimchi.

Pile a portion of kimchi into the centre of each plate, then pipe 5 blobs of mayo on top. Drizzle over a little extra olive oil, if you like.

Tarragon and wild garlic risotto with mushrooms and baked kombu potatoes

SERVES 4

50g salted butter
1 garlic clove, chopped
1 shallot, diced
200g risotto rice
50ml dry white wine
500ml vegetable stock
200g wild mushrooms, roughly torn
50g mascarpone
25g parmesan, grated
small bunch of tarragon, chopped
a few wild garlic leaves
sea salt and freshly ground
  black pepper

FOR THE POTATOES
150g new potatoes
1 parmesan rind
1 tablespoon kombu dried seaweed
pinch of sea salt

TO SERVE
2 tablespoons crème fraîche
a few micro herb sprigs or
  a few chives, chopped

In essence, this is of course two separate dishes. I wanted to serve the potatoes separately on the show, but little Sammy Head – the legend of the food team – couldn't be bothered to walk back down the mountain to get another bowl, so it became one dish! A great, simple risotto should be packed full of flavour; watch the seasoning as it usually needs more salt than you think and, whatever you do, don't make it too thick.

If using, light your BBQ. When the coals are silvery in colour, it's ready to cook on.

Heat the butter in a deep non-stick pan over a medium heat. Once the butter is melted and foaming, add the garlic, shallot and rice, stirring until the rice is well coated in the butter. Stir in the wine and around three-quarters of the stock, bring to the boil, then simmer for 15 minutes, stirring occasionally. Stir through the mushrooms and cook for a further 5 minutes until the rice is cooked and just tender.

Put the potatoes in a saucepan and cover with water, then add the parmesan rind, kombu seaweed and pinch of salt. Bring to the boil, then simmer for 15 minutes.

Drain the potatoes, then put them directly onto the grill bars of the BBQ and cook for 2–3 minutes, turning occasionally, until charred. Carefully lift out of the barbecue and set aside.

To finish the risotto, stir in the mascarpone, parmesan, tarragon (reserving a few sprigs for garnish), wild garlic and remaining stock, then season to taste. The texture should be slightly runny.

To serve, spoon the risotto onto 4 plates and garnish with a few extra sprigs of tarragon and micro herbs. Split the potatoes, top them with crème fraîche, micro herbs or chives and either serve on a separate plate alongside or place directly on top of the risotto.

Curried cauliflower and spring onions

SERVES 6

200ml thick Greek yogurt
1 tablespoon chilli powder
1 tablespoon garam masala
1 tablespoon ground cumin
1 large cauliflower, broken into
  large florets
8 spring onions, root ends trimmed

FOR THE SAUCE

25ml vegetable oil
2 onions, sliced
2 garlic cloves, crushed
1 tablespoon ginger paste
400g can chopped tomatoes
5 fresh tomatoes, chopped
sea salt and freshly ground
  black pepper
1 green and 1 red chilli, sliced
4 curry leaves
1 bay leaf
100ml double cream
50g salted butter

TO SERVE

handful of fresh coriander
  leaves, chopped
handful of toasted flaked almonds
naan breads

Penny and Allan started Transition Turriefield a few decades ago in order to become more self-sufficient. Visiting this little vegetable plot in Shetland makes you realise what can and can't be grown in this remote part of the UK. The weather plays a huge part but what is produced by these urban crofters is absolutely amazing, so much so that it's had a knock-on effect in the whole of Shetland: the government now offers discounted greenhouses that can be placed in people's gardens to encourage them to grow their own and reduce their carbon footprint. This dish was one of the tastiest on the trip, according to the crew!

Light your BBQ. When the coals are silvery in colour, it's ready to cook on.

First, make the sauce. Place a large flameproof pan on the BBQ (or over a medium heat on the hob). Add the oil and sliced onions, stir together and cook for 10 minutes until the onions are golden. Add the crushed garlic, ginger paste and both types of tomatoes, season well, and simmer for 5 minutes. Pour in 50ml water, add the chilli, the curry leaves and the bay leaf and cook for a further 2 minutes, then remove from the heat and set aside.

In a large bowl, mix the yogurt and spices together, then add the cauliflower florets and the spring onions, and turn until well coated in the marinade.

Secure the cauliflower florets and spring onions in a BBQ grilling basket, then BBQ until charred all over, turning the basket from time to time so that they cook evenly. Alternatively, place on a preheated griddle pan over a medium-high heat and grill, turning occasionally, until charred.

Return the pan to the heat (either on the BBQ or over a low-medium heat on the hob) and warm the sauce through. Stir in the cream and butter and taste to check the seasoning. Add the cauliflower and spring onions and cook for a further 3–4 minutes.

Serve, sprinkled with the coriander and flaked almonds, with naan breads on the side.

FISH & SHELLFISH

Burgh Island brill with beurre blanc

SERVES 4

2kg whole brill
sea salt and freshly ground
  black pepper
1 lemon, sliced into rounds

FOR THE BEURRE BLANC
1 shallot, diced
100ml dry white wine
6 black peppercorns
1 bay leaf
1 tablespoon white wine vinegar
25ml double cream
450g salted butter, diced
  and chilled
juice of ½ lemon
small bunch of chives, chopped

TO SERVE
120g mixed leaf salad, washed

The Burgh Island Hotel, perched on a private tidal island in South Devon, is an authentic throw-back to the Art Deco era. It's so impressive that, when you're inside, you feel as though you are on a film set for an Agatha Christie story. In fact, the author herself stayed on the island, writing two of her books there. On my visit, I just had to cook this dish, which is right up there for the right time, style of place and area.

Beurre blanc is a truly classic sauce that goes with any fish, but the local brill is amazing and so much cheaper than halibut or turbot.

Light your BBQ. When the coals are silvery in colour, it's ready to cook on.

To make the beurre blanc, put the shallot and wine into a medium saucepan, place over a high heat and bring to the boil. Add the peppercorns, bay leaf, vinegar and double cream (this helps to stabilise the sauce) and simmer until it reduces to around 2 tablespoons. Lift the peppercorns and bay out of the pan and discard. Take the pan off the heat and slowly whisk in the butter, a couple of pieces at a time, until the sauce has emulsified. Keep warm.

To prepare the brill, use a sharp pair of kitchen scissors to remove the fins, then cut off the head and tail using a sharp fish knife. Starting from the head, cut either side of the central bone to cut the brill into 2 halves. Place the portions onto a BBQ fish rack, season, then top with the lemon slices. Close the rack and cook on the BBQ for 4 minutes. Flip over and cook on the other side for a further 4 minutes.

Just before serving, finish the sauce with the lemon juice and stir in the chives. Spoon into a bowl.

Place the fish on a large warm platter, and serve with the beurre blanc and some mixed leaf salad.

PREVIOUS PAGE: LINDISFARNE, NORTHUMBERLAND
OPPOSITE: BURGH ISLAND, DEVON

Shetland's paella

SERVES 8

50ml olive oil

6 boneless chicken thighs

2 onions, sliced

3 garlic cloves, crushed

small bunch of oregano, thyme
  and marjoram, chopped

sea salt and freshly ground
  black pepper

150g paella rice

5 vine tomatoes, quartered

4 teaspoons smoked paprika

1 monkfish tail, cut into 2-cm pieces

16 whole shell-on prawns

8 scallops

300g mussels, cleaned and
  debearded (see tip)

small bunch of flat-leaf parsley,
  very finely chopped

This was the last dish I cooked on the trip and it really summed up the amazing produce they have in this part of the world, featuring both local fish and shellfish. I want to thank all the fishermen that brave the seas around these parts to deliver our catch – particularly Rob, who managed to get all this produce for me. I hope he enjoyed the dish, as I gave him not just the meal, but also the pan, the table... in fact everything on the last day of filming on location!

Light your BBQ. When the coals are silvery in colour, it's ready to cook on.

Place a 30-cm paella pan directly onto the BBQ or over a medium heat. Pour in half of the oil and fry the chicken thighs until golden all over. Add the onions, garlic and herbs, season well, then scatter the rice over the top. Stir once to combine, add the tomatoes, pour over 500ml cold water, then sprinkle over the paprika. Gently stir everything together and simmer for 20 minutes. Season again, then add all the fish. Drizzle the remaining oil over the top, cover with foil and cook for a further 10 minutes.

Remove the foil, discard any mussels that have not opened and sprinkle over the parsley just before serving.

JAMES'S TIP

Fresh mussels need to be alive before you cook them. To prepare them, pull off the stringy beards, knock off any barnacles and give the shells a scrub in fresh water to clean. Throw away ones with broken shells or any that don't close tightly when you tap them.

BAMBURGH CASTLE, NORTHUMBERLAND

Singapore crab with stottie cake

SERVES 6–8

200ml vegetable oil

2 whole garlic bulbs, cloves
    separated, peeled and sliced

1 red chilli, sliced

2 green chillies, sliced

2 bird's eye chillies, sliced

1 bunch of spring onions,
    trimmed and sliced

2 lemongrass stalks, chopped

10-cm piece fresh root ginger, diced

400ml tomato ketchup

100ml sweet chilli sauce

2 tablespoons caster sugar

50ml fish sauce

100ml soy sauce

100ml hoisin sauce

1 teaspoon smoked sea salt

16 cooked brown crab claws,
    shells cracked

2 cooked whole crabs, dead man's
    fingers removed, cut into 3 pieces

1 lobster, cooked, shell removed and
    cut into 6 pieces

small bunch of coriander, chopped

TO SERVE

small bunch of mint, chopped

bunch of spring onions, sliced

1 large stottie cake or ciabatta loaf,
    toasted and torn into chunks

When I visited the Northumberland Seafood Centre on the fabulous East Coast, I was fascinated to see the lobster hatchery and it gave me the idea for my favourite lobster and crab dish of all time. The wildlife around here shows you how rich the seas are, as I found out on a quick trip to Coquet Island to see the puffins. Next time you are in the area, I urge you to go and see it for yourself. I cooked the dish on the beach next to Bamburgh Castle and somehow the Singapore-style chilli sauce didn't seem out of place, mainly because no one else was there, which is crazy when you see how beautiful the coastline is. The local stottie cake loaf was great to mop up the leftover sauce.

If using, light your BBQ. When the coals are silvery in colour, it's ready to cook on. Line a large plate with kitchen paper.

Heat half of the vegetable oil in a small heavy saucepan placed over a medium heat or on the BBQ grill (use a flameproof pan if cooking on the BBQ) to 170°C/340°F or until a breadcrumb sizzles and turns brown when dropped into the oil. Fry the garlic in the hot oil for 1–2 minutes until golden and crisp, then remove with a slotted spoon to drain on the kitchen paper.

Put a large flameproof roasting tin over a medium heat on the hob, or onto the BBQ, and pour in the remaining oil. When the oil is hot, add the chillies, spring onions, lemongrass and ginger and fry for 1–2 minutes. Stir in the ketchup, sweet chilli sauce, caster sugar, fish sauce, soy and hoisin, season with the smoked sea salt and cook for a further 4 minutes.

Add all the crab and lobster to the roasting tin and stir through, making sure all the pieces are coated in the sauce. Cook for a further 4 minutes until heated through, then stir in the chopped coriander.

To serve, sprinkle over the mint, spring onions and crispy garlic and enjoy with chunks of toasted stottie cake or ciabatta to mop up the sauce.

Mussels in a cob with crispy cod cheeks

SERVES 2

FOR THE MUSSELS
25g salted butter
1 onion, diced
2 garlic cloves, chopped
2 celery sticks, diced
½ leek, diced
sea salt and freshly ground
  black pepper
a few sprigs of thyme
600g mussels, cleaned (see tip)
75ml dry white wine
100ml chicken stock
100ml double cream
small bunch of parsley, chopped
juice of 1 lemon

FOR THE COD CHEEKS
zest of 1 lemon
100g panko breadcrumbs
50g plain flour
2 eggs, beaten
6 cod cheeks
50g salted butter

TO SERVE
2 small cob loaves,
  hollowed out
small bunch of watercress

Mussels are a lot easier to get hold of than cod cheeks, which is a shame when you think of the amount of cod we eat. Why on earth does the best and tastiest part of it get thrown away? Cod cheeks are like the best fishfinger you will ever taste; a nugget of prized meat that wherever you go in France can be found even in supermarkets. So, come on Britain: demand the cod cheek!

Start by cooking the mussels. In a large saucepan with a lid, melt the butter over a medium heat. Add the onion, garlic, celery and leek, and cook for around 2 minutes until softened but without colouring. Season well, then add the thyme, mussels, wine and stock. Bring to the boil, cover and cook for 3 minutes until all the mussels have opened.

Rest a colander over a large bowl. Discard any mussels that still remain shut, then use a slotted spoon to lift the mussels out of the pan and into the colander. Let cool a little, then carefully remove the mussel meat from the shells, keeping a few whole ones in the shell for garnish.

Bring the sauce to the boil, uncovered, and cook until reduced by half. Pop all of the mussel meat back into the sauce along with any juices in the bowl, stir in the cream, reduce the heat to low and cook gently for 2 minutes, then add the parsley and lemon juice and season. Keep warm over a low heat while you cook the cod cheeks.

For the cod cheeks, mix the lemon zest and panko in a shallow dish. Put the flour into another dish and season well, then place the beaten eggs in another. Coat the cod cheeks first in the flour, then the egg and finally the breadcrumb mixture. Line a plate with kitchen paper.

Heat the butter in a frying pan over a medium heat. Once melted, add the cod cheeks and fry for 2 minutes, then flip over and cook for a further 2 minutes until golden. Drain on kitchen paper and season.

Put a hollowed-out cob on each plate and spoon in the mussels and sauce. Place the cod cheeks on top and garnish with the watercress.

JAMES'S TIP
Fresh mussels need to be alive before cooking. To prepare, pull off the stringy beards, knock off barnacles and scrub the shells in fresh water. Discard any with broken shells or that don't close tightly when tapped.

Clam vongole

SERVES 4

300g spaghetti
2 tablespoons olive oil
3 garlic cloves, chopped
1 shallot, diced
100ml dry white wine
1kg clams, cleaned (see tip)
sea salt and freshly ground
  black pepper
1 red chilli, diced
zest of 2 lemons,
  plus juice of 1 lemon
small bunch of parsley, chopped
50g parmesan, grated

Good clams can be found year-round on the coast all around Britain, but are at their best in the colder months. Clam vongole is simply the best pasta dish, in my opinion, but when made properly like Francesco Mazzei showed me, it's on a different level entirely.

Bring a large pan of salted water to the boil and cook the pasta, following the packet instructions, until al dente.

While the pasta's bubbling away, start the sauce. In a large saucepan with a lid, heat the oil over a medium heat, add the garlic and shallot and cook for 2 minutes, stirring often. Pour in the wine and clams, season well, then put the lid on the pan and bring to the boil. Reduce the heat a little and cook for a further 4 minutes.

Resting a colander over a bowl, use a large slotted spoon to lift the clams out of the sauce into the colander, then bring the sauce to the boil and simmer, uncovered, until reduced by half.

Drain the spaghetti and add it to the pan with the sauce and cook for a further 2 minutes.

Add the chilli, lemon zest and juice and parsley and season well. Stir everything together, then pop the clams back into the pan along with any of the juices caught in the bowl. Give everything a really big stir again to mix it all in, then scatter over the parmesan and drizzle in a little more olive oil, if you like. Serve immediately.

JAMES'S TIP
Fresh clams need to be alive before you cook them. To clean the clams of sand or grit, soak them for 20 minutes in a bowl of cold salty water. Drain, then transfer to a bowl of clean cold water to soak for a further 10 minutes, so they don't taste too salty.

Lobster omelette with lobster bisque

SERVES 2

1 cooked lobster, meat removed
    and shell reserved
10g salted butter

**FOR THE LOBSTER
BISQUE SAUCE**
1 medium tomato, chopped
25ml brandy
100ml double cream
15g salted butter

FOR THE VEGETABLES
25g salted butter
50g samphire
a few sea aster leaves,
    stalks removed

FOR THE OMELETTE
5 eggs, beaten
2 tablespoons double cream
sea salt and freshly ground
    black pepper
25g salted butter

Lobsters are expensive, so you really need to use every part of them – that means the shells as well as the meat. Enjoy this luxurious treat (the crew did).

Preheat the oven to 160°C (140°C fan)/325°F/gas 3.

Set the head, tail and claw shells of the lobster aside, then place all the soft shells into a medium saucepan to make the lobster bisque sauce. Pour in 100ml water, then add the tomato, brandy and cream. Bring to the boil over a medium heat, then simmer for 5 minutes.

Tip everything from the pan into the bowl of a food processor and blitz for 2–3 minutes. Strain the mixture through a fine sieve and into a clean saucepan. Whisk in the butter and heat gently to warm through.

For the vegetables, put the butter and a splash of water into a small saucepan set over a medium heat and add the samphire and sea aster leaves. Cover and cook for 1–2 minutes, then turn out onto a tray lined with a clean J-cloth.

Place the lobster tail and claw meat on the same tray, dot with the 10g of butter and transfer to the oven for a few minutes to warm through.

Slice the lobster tail and claw meat and set aside, then chop all the remaining meat.

To make the omelette, whisk the eggs and cream together in a bowl. Add the chopped lobster, season well and stir everything together.

Melt the butter in a large non-stick frying pan over a low-medium heat. As soon as the butter has melted and is foaming, pour in the egg mixture and tilt the pan so the mixture spreads over the base. When the mixture starts to firm up, use a fork to bring the edges of the mixture into the middle. Continue to cook the omelette until set but not coloured, then roll it up and transfer to a warm platter.

Arrange the sliced tail and claw meat on top of the omelette, spoon over the vegetables, then spoon over the sauce. Arrange the lobster head, tail and claw shells around the omelette to decorate, then serve.

Turbot on a boat

SERVES 6

2kg turbot
½ leek, thinly sliced
1 shallot, peeled and diced
2 sticks of celery, sliced
fronds from 1 fennel bulb
  (see sauce ingredients, below)
6 white peppercorns
a few sprigs of flat-leaf parsley
1 lemon, sliced
2 bay leaves

FOR THE SAUCE
50g salted butter
2 garlic cloves, sliced
1 shallot, diced
1 fennel bulb, thinly sliced
  (fronds reserved, see above)
sea salt and freshly ground
  black pepper
50ml Ricard pastis
500g mussels, cleaned
  (see tip)
200g clams, cleaned (see tip)
12 scallops, cleaned, roes removed
200ml double cream
small bunch of chives, chopped
small bunch of flat-leaf parsley,
  chopped
small bunch of dill, chopped
juice of ½ lemon

I would be lying if I said that the turbot we cooked on the boat, with its creamy shellfish and fennel sauce, was actually caught on the boat. The turbot weren't playing ball that day. The only thing we saw was terrible weather and the occasional ferry. However, the banter from the great skipper made up for the lack of fish.

Use a sharp filleting knife to remove the fins, head and tail from the turbot (alternatively, ask your fishmonger to do this for you).

Place the fish in a large flameproof roasting tin, at least 7cm deep. Pour in enough cold water to cover, then add the leek, shallot, celery, fennel fronds, peppercorns, parsley sprigs, sliced lemon and bay leaves. Bring to the boil, then simmer over a medium heat for 4–5 minutes.

Carefully lift the turbot onto a large warm plate. Strain the cooking liquor into a large bowl and set aside.

To make the sauce, heat the butter in the empty roasting tin over a low-medium heat. Once the butter is melted and foaming, stir in the garlic, shallot and sliced fennel, season, and cook for a few minutes, stirring occasionally, until softened. Pour in the pastis, then add the mussels, clams, scallops and cream. Season well and gently stir all the ingredients together. Bring to the boil, then simmer for 2–3 minutes.

Lift the fish back into the pan of sauce to warm through, then ladle in around 100ml of the cooking liquor and gently stir it in. Sprinkle over the chopped herbs, check the seasoning, then finish with the lemon juice before serving.

JAMES'S TIPS
Fresh mussels and clams need to be alive before you cook them. To prepare the mussels, pull off the stringy beards, knock off any barnacles and give the shells a scrub in fresh water to clean. Throw away any with broken shells or that don't close tightly when you tap them.

To clean the clams of sand or grit, soak them for 20 minutes in a bowl of cold salty water. Drain, then transfer to a bowl of clean cold water to soak for a further 10 minutes, so they don't taste too salty.

BBQ sea bream with Jersey Royals, deep-fried oysters and sauce vierge

SERVES 2

1 sea bream (about 750g), gutted
  and head and tail removed
1 lemon, sliced
small bunch of tarragon
small bunch of flat-leaf parsley
25ml olive oil
sea salt and freshly ground
  black pepper
150g Jersey Royals, cooked
  and sliced

FOR THE SAUCE
100ml olive oil
1 teaspoon coriander seeds,
  crushed
75g small Sunblush sundried
  tomatoes, drained
small bunch of flat-leaf parsley,
  chopped
small bunch of tarragon, chopped
a few sprigs of samphire,
  removed from woody stems

FOR THE OYSTERS
1 litre vegetable oil, for frying
50g plain flour
1 egg, beaten
50g panko breadcrumbs
8 pre-cooked oysters

For me, this was one of the best dishes of the entire trip! The deep-fried oysters with sauce vierge could be a dish on its own, but with the wonderful locally caught sea bream, cooked whole on the bone on a beach BBQ, it really couldn't get any better.

Light your BBQ. When the coals are silvery in colour, it's ready to cook on.

Place the sea bream inside a BBQ fish rack. Stuff the cavity with the lemon slices and herbs, drizzle with the oil and season well. Close the rack and cook on the BBQ for 4–5 minutes, then flip over and cook for a further 4–5 minutes until the fish is cooked through (you can test this by inserting a skewer into the fish – if it meets any resistance it is not ready yet).

Meanwhile, put all the ingredients for the sauce into a medium saucepan, season with salt and pepper and gently warm through on the BBQ or over a low-medium heat for 1–2 minutes.

Heat the vegetable oil for the oysters in a deep-fat fryer to 170°C/340°F or in a deep heavy-based saucepan until a breadcrumb sizzles and turns brown when dropped into it. (Note: hot oil can be dangerous; do not leave unattended.) Line a plate with kitchen paper.

Put the flour into one shallow bowl, the egg in another and the breadcrumbs in another. Season the flour well.

Dip the oysters first in the flour, then in the egg and lastly in the breadcrumbs to coat completely. Carefully lower into the hot oil and deep-fry for 30 seconds. Remove with a slotted spoon to drain on the kitchen paper and season with salt.

To serve, transfer the fish to a platter and place the potatoes around the outside. Spoon over the sauce and top with the deep-fried oysters.

Jersey Royal and squid ink 'risotto' with charred squid

SERVES 2

FOR THE SQUID
1 large squid
25ml olive oil
sea salt and freshly ground
   black pepper

FOR THE 'RISOTTO'
50g salted butter
1 shallot, diced
1 garlic clove, diced
50ml dry white wine
200ml chicken stock
2 teaspoons squid ink
200g Jersey Royal potatoes,
   chopped into very fine dice
1 tablespoon mascarpone
50g pecorino, grated

TO GARNISH
50g Jersey Royal pearl potatoes,
   cooked
15g salted butter
a few sprigs of samphire

This dish features the best potatoes in the business, Jersey Royals, which are unique to Jersey because of the soil and climate. Here, I used them to make a funky squid-ink risotto without rice… unusual, but it tastes amazing.

If using, light your BBQ. When the coals are silvery in colour, it's ready to cook on.

To prepare the squid, put it on a board and remove the membrane from the body, then pull out the tentacles. Remove and discard the cartilage from inside the body. Wipe the body inside and out to clean it. Cut the tentacles away from the eyes and discard this bit. Cut the body into strips or rings. Drizzle these, and the tentacles, in a little oil and season, then set aside.

Heat two-thirds of the butter for the risotto in a non-stick saucepan over a medium heat or on the BBQ. Once the butter is melted and foaming, stir in the shallot and garlic and cook for 2–3 minutes until softened, without letting them colour. Pour in the wine and stock and bring to the boil, then stir in the squid ink and diced potatoes. Season well and simmer for 5 minutes.

Meanwhile, cook the squid on the BBQ for 2 minutes – it will only need a few minutes and will still have a lovely tender texture. Alternatively, cook the squid on a preheated griddle pan over a high heat. Lift off and rest on a clean board for 1 minute.

Put the Jersey Royal pearl potatoes for the garnish in a small pan, along with the butter and samphire, and warm through until hot.

To finish the risotto, drain away any excess liquid, then stir in the mascarpone and pecorino. Check the seasoning, then stir through the remaining butter.

To serve, spoon the risotto onto plates, top with the squid and spoon over the Jersey Royal pearls, samphire and the buttery juices.

Isles of Scilly pollock with a bean and tomato stew

SERVES 4

4 x 150-g pollock fillets, skin on
sea salt and freshly ground
  black pepper
50g salted butter

FOR THE STEW
1 tablespoon olive oil
2 garlic cloves, sliced
1 shallot, diced
1 small fennel bulb, half diced
  and half thinly sliced
12 cherry tomatoes, halved
2 large heritage tomatoes, diced
50g Sunblush sundried tomatoes
  in oil, chopped
50ml dry white wine
400g can haricot beans, drained
small handful of rock samphire
small handful of sea beets or
  baby spinach
15g salted butter

Pollock is deemed the poor man's haddock or cod, which is sad in a way, as there is plenty of it and it's a great-tasting fish. Slightly salting it for ten minutes before cooking will firm it up and makes it easier to cook with. I used some of the great sea salt that is produced all around Cornwall for this and created a simple bean and tomato stew to go with it.

Put the fish onto a tray and sprinkle over 2 tablespoons of sea salt. Leave for 10 minutes, then wash off and pat dry.

To make the stew, heat a non-stick saucepan over a medium heat. Pour in the oil, then stir in the garlic, shallot and all of the fennel and cook for 2–3 minutes until starting to soften. Add all the tomatoes, along with a spoonful of oil from the sundried tomatoes, and stir everything together. Pour in the wine, bring to the boil, then stir in the beans and cook gently for 10 minutes.

To cook the fish, heat a non-stick frying pan over a medium heat until hot, then add the 50g butter. Once the butter is melted and foaming, slide the fish into the pan, flesh-side down. Cook for 2 minutes, then flip over and cook for a further 2 minutes. Season on each side.

Finish the stew by stirring through the samphire, sea beets or baby spinach and butter. Taste to check the seasoning, adding more salt and pepper if needed.

To serve, spoon the stew onto a large warm platter and top with the fish.

Yorkshire-tea-smoked trout with sauce gribiche and rhubarb

SERVES 2

90g long grain rice
60g demerara sugar
30g Yorkshire tea leaves
1 x 300-g trout, gutted,
  cleaned and head removed
olive oil, for drizzling

FOR THE CROUTONS
1–2 tablespoons olive oil
3 slices of white bread,
  crusts removed and bread
  diced into 1-cm cubes

FOR THE GRIBICHE SAUCE
cooked yolks of 2 hard-boiled eggs
50ml olive oil, plus extra
  for drizzling
1 tablespoon Dijon mustard
zest and juice of 1 lemon
1 large new potato (about 50g),
  cooked and finely diced
small mixed bunch of parsley,
  tarragon and chives, chopped,
  with a few parsley sprigs reserved
  to garnish
1 shallot, finely diced
2 gherkins, diced
2 tablespoons capers
sea salt and freshly ground
  black pepper

TO SERVE
1 stick of rhubarb

This trout came from the lake that sits on the Coniston Country Estate in Yorkshire, where the crew were staying. The technique of hot tea smoking is a great way to cook it. This was one of the many places we visited where the crew returned with their families after filming had finished, to experience the beautiful Yorkshire Dales for a little longer.

Preheat a griddle pan over a high heat. Alternatively, light your BBQ. When the coals are silvery in colour, it's ready to cook on.

Mix the rice, sugar and tea leaves in a bowl. Tear off a large piece of foil measuring around 50 x 20cm. Pour the rice mixture on top and spread out slightly so it lies in an even layer. Fold over the edges and seal to make a tight flat parcel, then use a knife to pierce several holes in the top of the parcel.

Tear another large piece of foil, again measuring around 50 x 20cm. Put the tea parcel in the middle, then lay the trout on top of it. Drizzle some oil over the trout, then enclose it completely in the foil. Ensuring the tea parcel is on the bottom, place on the hot griddle pan or grill of the BBQ for 5–6 minutes.

While the fish is smoking, make the croutons. Heat a large non-stick frying pan over a medium-high heat until hot, add the oil, then fry the bread cubes until golden and crisp, turning regularly. Remove with a slotted spoon to drain on kitchen paper.

To make the sauce, whisk the egg yolks, oil and mustard together in a bowl. Whisk in the lemon zest and juice, then add the cooked potato cubes, herbs, shallot, gherkins and capers. Season well and mix together.

To serve, take the trout parcel off the heat and unwrap it. Lift the trout onto a large platter and peel away and discard the skin on the top fillet. Spoon the sauce around the edges, drizzle over a little more oil and scatter around the reserved parsley sprigs and the croutons. Finally, use a potato peeler to shave the rhubarb in thin curls over the top.

Monkfish and mussels with tomato and ginger sauce

SERVES 4

500g mussels, cleaned and
  debearded (see tip on page 80)

50ml white wine

75g salted butter

1 teaspoon garam masala

10-cm piece fresh root ginger,
  grated

3 garlic cloves, crushed

1 shallot, diced

12 large tomatoes, skinned,
  deseeded and diced

sea salt and freshly ground
  black pepper

1kg monkfish tail

1 lemon, sliced

small bunch of dill, chopped

small bunch of flat-leaf parsley,
  chopped

The sauce for this is a great combination that works with any seafood, and – let's face it – this country is surrounded with so much to choose from. I love a simple piece of monkfish, but also serve this with cod in the restaurant. Either way, use fresh ginger, grated skin-on, if you want to warm the sauce up even more. Shetland and the north coast of Scotland have the best monkfish you can get – when cooked, it's whiter than white. In recent years, chefs have liked it too much, so the price has increased, but when you can find it, buy it!

Light your BBQ. When the coals are silvery, it's ready to cook on.

Put the mussels and wine in a large flameproof pan, cover with a lid and cook for 3–4 minutes on the BBQ (or on the hob over a medium heat) until all the mussels have opened. Strain through a colander resting over a bowl to reserve the liquor (no need to wash the pan – it's needed to make the spiced butter). Discarding any mussels that are still shut, pick the mussel meat from about half of the shells and set aside.

Add 50g of the butter and the garam masala to the mussel pan, then return to the heat to melt the butter. Stir together and set aside.

In a separate pan, melt the remaining 25g of butter. When it is foaming, stir in the ginger, garlic, shallot and tomatoes, and cook for 2–3 minutes until beginning to soften. Season, then add the reserved cooking liquor from the mussels, pouring it through a fine sieve to catch any sediment.

Cut the monkfish tail two-thirds of the way through the middle and fill with the lemon slices, herbs and picked mussel meat. Tie the tail with string to enclose the stuffing, then thread the monkfish onto 2 metal skewers down the length of the tail. Place on the BBQ and roast for 10–12 minutes, turning it and brushing it with the spiced butter from time to time. Alternatively cook on a preheated griddle over a high heat. Once cooked, remove the skewers and cut off the string.

To serve, spoon the tomato and ginger sauce onto a platter and sit the monkfish on top, then arrange the mussels in their shells around the outside.

Korean seabass with BBQ baby aubergines

SERVES 6

1.5kg line-caught seabass
10 baby aubergines
olive oil
sea salt and freshly ground
 black pepper
6 spring onions, sliced diagonally
200g clams, cleaned
 (see tip on page 80)
300g mussels, cleaned and
 debearded (see tip on page 80)
zest and juice of 1 lime
a few sprigs of mint and coriander
sesame oil, for drizzling

FOR THE SAUCE
2 tablespoons gochujang chilli paste
4 tablespoons soy sauce
2 teaspoons sesame oil
6 tablespoons soft brown sugar
5-cm piece fresh root ginger, grated
4 garlic cloves, crushed
1 green chilli, diced
1 tablespoon each white and
 black sesame seeds
zest and juice of 1 lime
1 tablespoon freshly chopped mint
1 tablespoon freshly chopped
 coriander

I cooked this dish in Poole Harbour, the second-largest natural harbour in the world after Sydney. The area is famous for its cockles and seabass. This simple sauce goes well with any fish but also meat, such as chicken, beef or lamb. With the view of exclusive Sandbanks behind us, I was lucky not to stain the boat, but I was assured it was 'only' worth 4 million quid, which wouldn't buy you a garage around here.

Light your BBQ. When the coals are silvery, it's ready to cook on.

 Put the seabass on a board and use a sharp fish knife to cut under the gills, then slide your knife into the flesh of the fish to start to remove the fillet. Working along the backbone and, keeping the fish knife flat, carefully continue to cut the fish away from the backbone and rib cage to remove the fillet. Turn the fish over and repeat on the other side to remove the other fillet. Set aside.

Place all the ingredients for the sauce, apart from the lime zest and juice and the herbs, into a small pan over a low heat. Season well and cook gently for 2–3 minutes. Sprinkle in half of the herbs, season well and stir, then simmer the sauce gently for a couple of minutes. Add the lime zest and juice, stir again, then take the pan off the heat.

Meanwhile, pop the aubergines onto a board and drizzle a little olive oil over each one, season and rub in. Lift onto the BBQ rack and cook for about 8 minutes, turning a couple of times until roasted all over. As soon as they're ready, lift them onto a large serving dish.

 Tear a large square piece of foil, big enough to enclose the fish, and lay on a board. Sprinkle over a third of the spring onions, pop the bass fillets on top, then add the clams and mussels. Spoon about 4 tablespoons of the sauce over the fish. Sprinkle over the lime zest, the juice and another third of the spring onions, plus the mint and coriander sprigs. Pop another piece of foil over the top and seal the edges well. Place the parcel onto the BBQ and cook for 4–5 minutes.

 Open the parcel, check that the fish is opaque and the clams and mussels have opened (discard any that remain shut), then arrange over the aubergines. Spoon over the remaining sauce and sprinkle over the last spring onions. Finally, drizzle over a little sesame oil and serve.

Wasabi mountain salmon

SERVES 4–6

400g fresh salmon fillet,
  skinned and thinly sliced
50ml sesame oil

**FOR THE DEEP-FRIED
SPRING ONIONS**
1–2 litres vegetable oil, for frying
100g cornflour
125ml sparkling water
6 large spring onions, whites only,
  roots attached

FOR THE DRESSING
¼ teaspoon fresh grated wasabi
1 teaspoon yuzu juice
50ml dark soy sauce
juice of 1 lime

TO SERVE
1 teaspoon mixed white and
  black sesame seeds, toasted
1 tablespoon mixed micro herbs
  (such as red amaranth, mizuna,
  micro coriander and red shiso)

Wasabi is highly prized and expensive and takes over two years to grow. On my trip, I discovered that there are only a handful of wasabi growers outside Japan and Wasabi Crop in Northern Ireland is one of them. Dr. Sean Kitson and his son Zak produce fantastic wasabi in County Armagh in the grounds of their house. I'd never seen it grown, let alone tasted it (I have never even been into horseradish – for me, it's the devil's food), but this stuff was amazing. Do buy some, although there could be a waiting list as it's so popular. I wish them all the best as a new-found fan. The key to fresh wasabi, once grated, is to let it air for a while before using. Do also use the freshest salmon you can find for this dish as it is only very lightly cooked by the hot-oil dressing.

Heat the vegetable oil for the spring onions in a deep-fat fryer to 180°C/350°F or in a deep heavy-based saucepan until a breadcrumb sizzles and turns brown when dropped into it. (Note: hot oil can be dangerous; do not leave unattended.) Line a large plate with kitchen paper.

While the oil is heating up, prepare the dressing. Put all the ingredients into a bowl and mix together. Set aside.

Whisk together the cornflour and sparkling water in a large bowl – don't worry if the batter consistency is thin, that is how it should be.

To prepare the spring onions, carefully slice each one from the root to the top 6 times, ensuring you keep the root-end intact. Dip each one into the batter and fry in batches for 30 seconds until crisp. Lift out with a slotted spoon to drain on the kitchen paper.

Lay the salmon slices over a large platter. In a small pan, heat the sesame oil until hot and almost smoking, then spoon it over the salmon, followed by the dressing. Sprinkle over the sesame seeds, then top with the deep-fried spring onions and micro herbs.

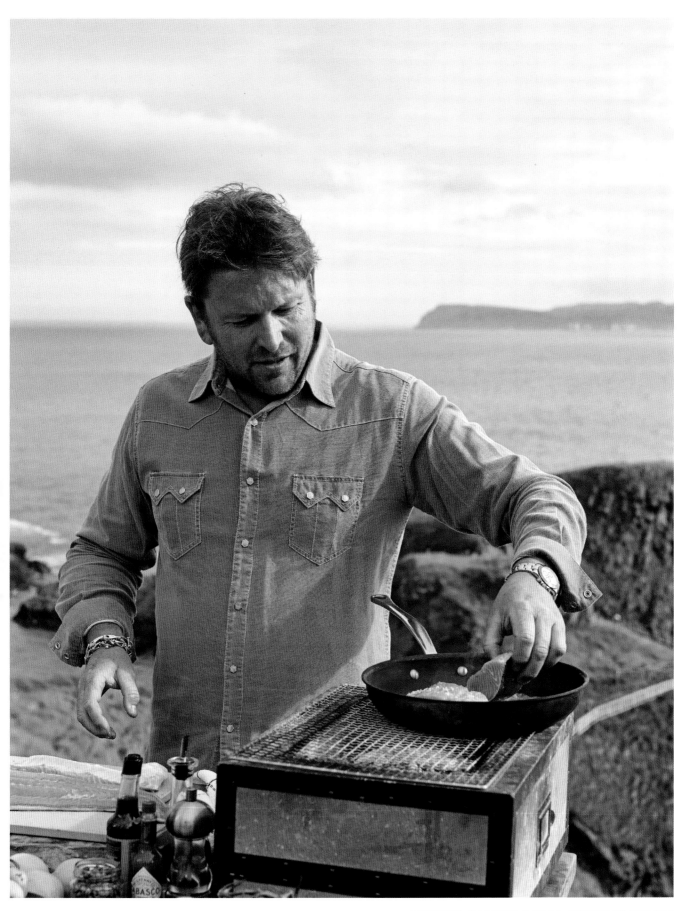

OPPOSITE: CARRICK-A-REDE, NORTHERN IRELAND

Irish salmon with mussels

SERVES 2

50g salted butter

1 tablespoon olive oil

2 x 200-g salmon portions

sea salt and freshly ground
   black pepper

½ shallot, diced

½ garlic clove, sliced

a few sprigs of fresh tarragon

2 large new potatoes,
   cooked and diced

2 large tomatoes, skinned,
   deseeded and finely chopped

200g fresh mussels, cleaned and
   debearded (see tip)

1 tablespoon capers

1 tablespoon Worcestershire sauce

½ teaspoon Tabasco sauce

juice of ½ lemon

I've learnt a lot on this trip: some good, some bad, but all stories to help us understand food and drink better. The decline of the Atlantic salmon is one of the saddest stories of them all, as I found out on my visit to the Carrick-a-Rede rope bridge in Northern Ireland. Suspended almost 30 metres above sea level, it was first erected in 1755 by salmon fishermen to reach the small island where they fished for Atlantic salmon at the point they paused before entering the rivers to spawn. Sadly, the final fish was caught here in 2002. Cheap salmon and the people that produce it should be outlawed, as they are directly responsible for the massive decline of wild salmon in recent years. Cheap farmed salmon is not only cheap, it's also bad for your health. My advice is always to buy the best salmon you can from the most sustainable producers.

Heat a large, deep frying pan over a medium heat until hot, then add half the butter and the oil. As soon as the butter has melted and is foaming, place the salmon into the pan, skin-side down, and season well. Cook for 2–3 minutes, then flip over and cook for a further 2 minutes. Lift off and place onto a warm plate.

   Pour away most of the fat from the pan, then place the pan back on the heat and add the remaining butter. Stir in the shallot, garlic and tarragon and sauté for 1–2 minutes. Add the potatoes, tomatoes, mussels, capers, Worcestershire sauce and Tabasco. Season well and stir until well combined. Pop a lid on and cook for 2 minutes until all the mussels have opened (discard any that are still shut).

   To finish, squeeze over the lemon juice, then spoon into bowls and top with the salmon.

JAMES'S TIP

Fresh mussels need to be alive before you cook them. To prepare them, pull off the stringy beards, knock off any barnacles and give the shells a scrub in fresh water to clean. Throw away ones with broken shells or any that don't close tightly when you tap them.

Lough Neagh eels, two ways, with bacon and butter sauce

SERVES 6

FOR THE BBQ EEL AND POLLAN FISH

3 x 100-g pieces fresh eel

3 x 150–200-g pollan fish (or mackerel or herring if unavailable), gutted and scaled

FOR THE FISHCAKE BALLS

1–2 litres vegetable oil, for deep-frying

300g cooked potatoes, riced

1 egg yolk, plus 2 eggs, beaten

2 spring onions, thinly sliced

200g smoked eel fillets, flaked

75g plain flour

100g panko breadcrumbs

FOR THE SAUCE

1 tablespoon vegetable oil

100g bacon lardons

1 shallot, finely diced

sea salt and freshly ground black pepper

50ml dry white wine

300g chilled salted butter, cubed

25ml double cream

juice of ½ lemon

2 tablespoons chopped fresh chives

FOR THE GARNISH

1 tablespoon salted butter

12 Savoy cabbage leaves, thinly sliced

50g soup celery, thinly sliced (optional)

Lough Neagh is the largest lake in the British Isles, famous for its fantastic eels and pollan, which is a type of freshwater herring. We got a chance to see how difficult food like this is to harvest. The eels are caught on a massive 400-hook line and pulled in by hand. It was a unique sight and one of the highlights of my trip.

Light your BBQ. When the coals are silvery, it's ready to cook on.

Start with the sauce. In a medium saucepan, heat the oil until hot, then stir in the bacon and fry until crisp. Stir in the shallot, season and cook for 1 minute, then pour in the wine. As soon as the wine comes to the boil, take the pan off the heat and whisk in the butter, a couple of cubes at a time, then whisk in the double cream. Season, then add the lemon juice and chives and stir everything together. Set aside.

Heat the oil for the fishcakes in a deep-fat fryer to 170°C/340°F or in a deep heavy-based saucepan until a breadcrumb sizzles and turns brown when dropped into it. (Note: hot oil can be dangerous; do not leave unattended.) Line a large plate with kitchen paper.

To make the fishcake balls, put the potato, egg yolk, spring onions and smoked eel into a large bowl. Season and fold together gently. Put the flour into a shallow bowl and season. Put the beaten eggs into another bowl and the breadcrumbs into another.

Take one-sixth of the fishcake mixture and roll into a ball. Coat it first in the flour, then the egg and finally the breadcrumbs. Repeat this process until you've used up the mixture. Fry the balls in batches in the vegetable oil for 3–4 minutes. Lift out with a slotted spoon to drain on the kitchen paper and season with salt.

Drizzle a little oil over the fresh eel and pollan and season. Pop onto the BBQ and cook for 3–4 minutes, turning halfway. You can also cook them in a roasting tin in an oven preheated to 200°C (180°C fan)/ 400°F/gas 6 for 6–8 minutes.

Place the garnish ingredients into a medium saucepan set over a medium heat. Season well and cook for around 2 minutes.

Meanwhile, gently reheat the sauce over a low heat.

To serve, spoon half of the sauce onto a large warm platter, top with half of the cabbage mixture, then arrange over the fish and eel pieces. Spoon the remaining sauce into the centre of 6 separate plates, top with a nest of the cabbage mixture, then top each with a fishcake ball.

Skate with brown butter sauce

SERVES 2

1 tablespoon plain flour
sea salt and freshly ground
    black pepper
2 x 250-g skate wings, cleaned
2 tablespoons vegetable oil
large handful of watercress,
    to garnish

FOR THE BROWN BUTTER SAUCE
150g Welsh salted butter, diced
2 tablespoons nonpareille capers
juice of 1 lemon, plus 1 lemon,
    peeled and cut into segments
small bunch of flat-leaf parsley,
    chopped

This is one of the best-looking dishes and the tastiest, but sadly overfishing and the use of trawlers has all but destroyed the UK skate stocks. Nets are the issue: scooping up all ages and sizes of fish. As a result, I will only buy line-caught skate from day boats around the UK. For me, this is one of the best fish you can try.

Preheat the oven to 200°C (180°C fan)/400°F/gas 6.

Tip the flour onto a plate and season well. Dip each skate wing into the seasoned flour to coat on both sides, then dust off any excess.

Heat the oil in a large ovenproof frying pan over a medium heat. Once hot, lay the skate in the pan and cook for 2 minutes, then flip each wing over and transfer the pan to the oven for 4 minutes until cooked through. Check by inserting the tip of a sharp knife – the fish should be opaque all the way through.

Meanwhile, make the sauce. Melt the butter in a large heavy-based pan over a medium heat until it turns a nutty brown and smells toasty. Immediately add the capers, lemon juice, lemon segments and parsley and season well. Swirl the pan around to mix everything together.

To serve, put each skate wing onto a plate, spoon over the brown butter sauce and garnish with watercress.

Cod with warm tartare sauce and oyster fritters

SERVES 2

2 x 150-g cod fillets, skinned
sea salt and freshly ground
  black pepper
1 tablespoon vegetable oil
15g salted butter

FOR THE SAUCE

1 teaspoon vegetable oil
½ shallot, finely diced
100ml double cream
2 tablespoons fresh or
  good-quality mayonnaise
4 cornichons, diced
1 teaspoon nonpareille capers
a few sprigs of dill and parsley,
  chopped
juice of ¼ lemon

FOR THE OYSTER FRITTERS

1 litre vegetable oil, for deep-frying
50g plain flour
50ml sparkling water
pinch of salt
4 freshly shucked oysters

A classic combination, whether served hot or cold. Did you know that if you make your own mayonnaise or use good-quality fresh mayonnaise, you can actually warm it up into a sauce? Don't try to make it work with the inferior stuff, as the sauce will split.

Preheat the oven to 200°C (180°C fan)/400°F/gas 6.

Season the cod with salt and pepper. Heat a non-stick ovenproof frying pan over a medium heat until hot. Add the oil and fry the cod for 2–3 minutes. Flip the cod over, add half the butter to the pan and transfer to the oven to cook for a further 2–3 minutes. Take the pan out of the oven, add the remaining butter and let it melt, then spoon it over the fish. Set aside to rest while you make the sauce.

Heat the oil for the sauce in a small saucepan over a medium heat, then add the shallot and cook for 2–3 minutes until just softened. Add the cream and bring to the boil, then reduce to a simmer and stir in the mayonnaise, cornichons, capers, chopped herbs and lemon juice. Season to taste.

Meanwhile, heat the oil for the fritters in a deep-fat fryer to 190°C/375°F or in a deep heavy-based saucepan until a breadcrumb sizzles and turns brown when dropped into it. (Note: hot oil can be dangerous; do not leave unattended.) Line a plate with kitchen paper.

To make a batter for the oysters, whisk together the flour, water and salt in a small bowl. Dip each oyster in the mixture until coated, then carefully lower into the hot oil. Fry for 1 minute until golden and crisp. Lift out with a slotted spoon to drain on the kitchen paper and sprinkle with salt.

To serve, spoon the sauce between 2 serving plates, then top with the fish and the oyster fritters.

Salt-baked seabass with an edible flower salad

SERVES 6

500g plain flour,
  plus extra for dusting
4 large egg whites
700g sea salt, fine or coarse
a few sprigs of thyme, leaves picked
1 x 3-kg seabass, scaled and gutted,
  with fins, head and tail removed

FOR THE SALAD
1 tablespoon Dijon mustard
1 tablespoon white wine vinegar
50ml vegetable oil
sea salt and freshly ground
  black pepper
a selection of salad leaves and
  edible flowers

TO SERVE
lemon wedges

Cornish salt is the key to this dish – the salt flavours the fish and it steams inside its own case. I was also inspired by the great seabass I get from Jimmy at Flying Fish, a place we visited on the last series. Based in Cornwall, they deliver to most of the best restaurants in the UK. On my visit to the Isles of Scilly, I learnt that it was famous for its cut flowers that were sent to the mainland, so I decided to marry this dish up with an edible flower salad – it makes a great combination. You could also use smaller fish, such as trout or farmed seabass, but reduce the cooking time accordingly.

Preheat the oven to 200°C (180°C fan)/400°F/gas 6 and line a large baking tray with baking parchment.

Combine the flour, egg whites, salt and thyme in a large bowl and pour in 200ml cold water. Mix everything together by hand to make a smooth dough. Cut the dough in half and roll each piece out on a clean work surface dusted with a little flour to form 2 large rectangles, around 5mm thick and slightly larger than the piece of fish.

Place the fish on top of one of the rectangles of pastry dough and brush the edges with water. Cover with the other rectangle of dough and press down around the fish to seal. Trim off any excess dough, leaving a 1-cm border, then lift onto the lined tray.

Brush the dough all over with water and bake for 40 minutes.

Whisk the mustard, vinegar and oil for the salad dressing together in a large bowl with 1 tablespoon of water, then season and whisk again. Add the salad leaves and flowers and toss together.

To serve the seabass, cut away the crust with a knife and pull away and discard the skin, lift the fish onto plates and serve with a pile of salad and lemon wedges for squeezing.

Octopus and chorizo stew

SERVES 6

50ml olive oil
2 garlic cloves, sliced
1 onion, diced
1 leek, sliced
a sprig of rosemary, chopped
a few sprigs of thyme
2 celery sticks, diced
1 bay leaf
200ml dry white wine
400g can chopped tomatoes
400g chorizo, sliced
sea salt and freshly ground
    black pepper
1 octopus, frozen and
    thawed to tenderise
1–2 x 400g cans butter beans,
    drained
25g salted butter
large bunch of flat-leaf parsley,
    chopped

A classic combination and one you see in many restaurants and cafés in the Mediterranean, so why not in the UK? The Yorkshire chorizo that Brian Turner sourced for me is amazing in this and the octopus adds so much flavour to the bean stew as it cooks; it's a winner. Be careful with the salt though: you only need to add a little at the end.

Heat half of the olive oil in a large saucepan over a medium heat, add the garlic, onion, leek, rosemary, thyme, celery and bay leaf and cook for 2 minutes until just starting to soften. Stir in the wine, bring to the boil, then add the chopped tomatoes and chorizo and season well. Pop in the octopus, cover with a lid and cook over a gentle heat for 1 hour.

Lift the octopus out of the stew and onto a board. Tip the beans into the pan, stir and bring to the boil. Stir in the butter and parsley and season again.

Slice the tentacles from the octopus (discard the head) and drizzle with the remaining olive oil. Heat a griddle pan until hot, then cook the tentacles, turning occasionally, until charred all over.

Serve the stew topped with the octopus.

Lovage-crusted plaice on the bone with buttered new potatoes

SERVES 2

1 large plaice
2 tablespoons olive oil,
  plus a little extra for greasing

FOR THE HERB CRUST
large bunch of lovage
large bunch of flat-leaf parsley
2 thick slices of bread, with crusts,
  roughly chopped
sea salt and freshly ground
  black pepper
zest of 1 lemon and juice of ½ lemon
50g grated parmesan
50g full-fat cream cheese

TO SERVE
300g new potatoes, halved if large
25g salted butter

I just love plaice; to me it's one of the finest fish when fresh. Try signing up for the fish box schemes that are now available. Using the same idea as veg boxes, fishmongers and fishermen will now deliver the best fresh fish to your door overnight. This crust will also work with any fish that might arrive in the box.

Preheat the oven to 180°C (160°C fan)/350°F/gas 4 and line a baking sheet with baking parchment.

To prepare the plaice, put the fish on a board and use scissors to trim off the tail and all the outer fins around the body, starting from the tail and working up towards the head. Remove the head by using a sharp fish knife to cut around and behind the fin to separate the head from the body. When you reach the hard bone at the top of the head, tap the knife gently with a hammer to cut through it. Take a clean J-cloth and wipe out and remove all of the bloodline inside the cavity of the fish, then cut the fish in half lengthways. You can remove the skin, too, but this is optional. Place the fish onto the lined baking sheet.

For the crust, put the herbs into the bowl of a large food processor and whiz to finely chop, then add the bread and whiz again to chop it into fine breadcrumbs. Season the mixture, then add the lemon zest and juice and both types of cheese. Whiz again to bring everything together to a paste.

Line a board with a sheet of baking parchment and spoon the crust mixture on top. Lay a sheet of clingfilm over the top and flatten, then roll out until the mixture is around 2mm thick. Remove the clingfilm and upturn the crust onto the fish. Gently remove the paper, then cover the crust in clingfilm again and smooth down over the fish to completely cover it. Remove the clingfilm and drizzle the olive oil over the top. Roast for 15–20 minutes until the fish is opaque and easily lifts away from the bone when tested with the tip of a knife.

Meanwhile, cook the potatoes in a pan of boiling salted water for around 15 minutes until tender. Drain well and return to the pan. Add the butter, season, then cover the pan with a lid to keep warm.

Lift the fish onto a warmed platter and spoon the potatoes into a bowl to serve.

Double Shetland cod with tomato ragout

SERVES 2–3

FOR THE TOMATO RAGOUT
100g salt cod, soaked in cold
   water overnight
100g dried piltock (saithe/coley),
   soaked in cold water overnight
5 tablespoons olive oil
1 shallot, diced
3 garlic cloves, crushed
300g heritage tomatoes, chopped
50ml dry white wine,
   plus extra if necessary
small bunch of basil,
   leaves picked and torn
sea salt and freshly ground
   black pepper
100g cooked potatoes, diced
100g cooked white beans
   (cannellini or haricot), drained
small bunch of flat-leaf parsley,
   chopped

FOR THE FRESH COD
1 tablespoon olive oil
25g salted butter
2–3 x 200-g cod fillets

Thule Ventus, producing Shetland air-dried salt cod in the village of Cunningsburgh, has to be one of the smallest places we went to see on the trip, but what it lacked in size it made up for in flavour. The sustainably caught fish is cured, dried and packed over a two-month period in a small shed with a stunning view of the island and coast. Piltock is coley that is treated in the same way as the cod and has a better taste, if you ask me. Both the dried piltock and salt cod can be bought online. Soak it overnight in cold water and cook simply, as they do locally, in water or milk. It's worth trying.

Drain the salt cod and piltock of their soaking water and wash in fresh water. Put in a pan, cover with fresh cold water and bring slowly to the boil. Simmer for 5 minutes, then lift onto a plate to cool. Use a fork to flake the fish, while picking over and removing the bones.

Preheat the oven to 180°C (160°C fan)/350°F/gas 4.

Heat 2 tablespoons of the olive oil in a large pan and gently fry the shallot and garlic for 2–3 minutes until just starting to soften. Stir in the tomatoes and cook for 2 minutes. Pour in the wine and add half the basil and season. Stir together and cook for 8–10 minutes over a low heat until the ingredients have cooked down to make a stew. If the pan looks a little dry, add a splash more wine.

To cook the fresh cod, heat an ovenproof non-stick frying pan until hot and add the olive oil and half of the butter. Once the butter is melted and foaming, fry the cod, skin-side down, for 2 minutes. Season lightly and when the skin has turned golden, carefully flip over and transfer to the oven to cook for 3–4 minutes. Remove from the oven and add the remaining butter to the pan. Once melted, spoon over the cod.

To finish the stew, add the potatoes, beans and flaked salted fish and stir everything gently together. Season with a pinch of salt and plenty of black pepper. Stir in the remaining 3 tablespoons of olive oil, the remaining basil and the parsley.

Divide the ragout among the plates, place the cod on top and serve.

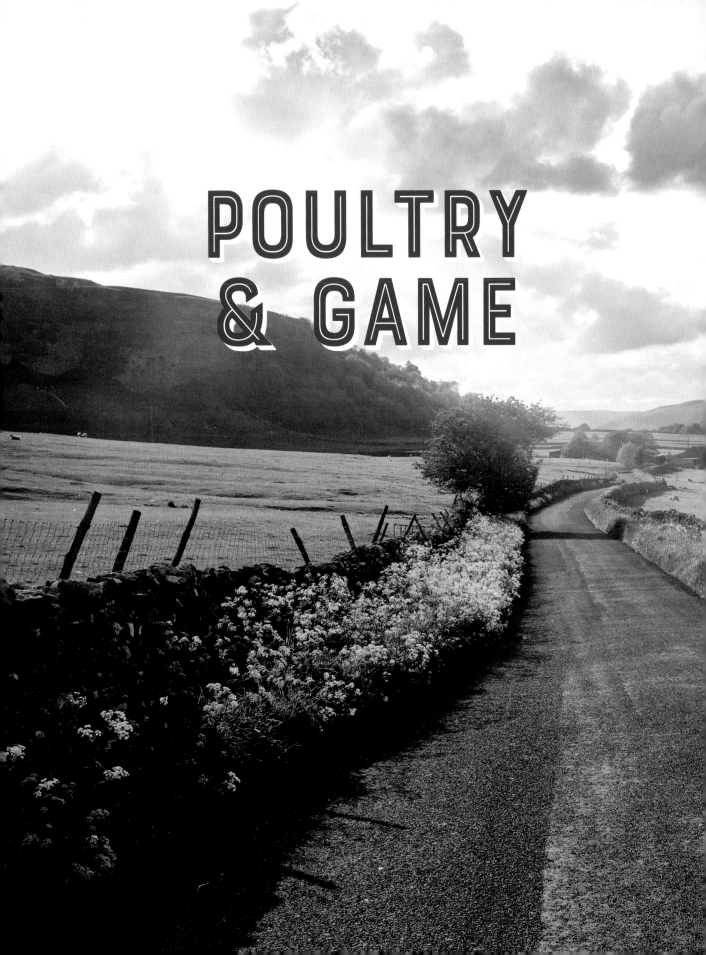

POULTRY
& GAME

Lemon and herb chicken with dhal

SERVES 4

1 x 2-kg chicken,
  jointed into 8 pieces
2 lemons, sliced
small bunch of mint
small bunch of coriander
50ml olive oil
sea salt and freshly ground
  black pepper

FOR THE DHAL
50g salted butter
1 medium onion, diced
6 curry leaves
1 tablespoon black mustard seeds
1 tablespoon ready-made
  ginger purée or paste
1 tablespoon ready-made
  garlic purée or paste
1 teaspoon turmeric
1 teaspoon ground cumin
1 teaspoon ground coriander
1 teaspoon garam masala
200g red lentils

TO SERVE
1 tablespoon chopped
  fresh coriander
1 tablespoon chopped fresh mint

As a nation, we love Indian flavours and here they are combined in a great dish that's quick to cook and tasty to eat. You can get chicken anywhere, but in the Lake District I chose to use the amazing Goosnargh Chicken from neighbouring Lancashire. This corn-fed chicken is not intensively farmed and I really think it is the best you can get.

Light your BBQ. When the coals are silvery in colour, it's ready to cook on.

Heat half of the butter for the dhal in a medium saucepan placed over a medium heat or onto the rack of the BBQ. Once the butter has melted, stir in the onions and fry for around 10 minutes until starting to turn golden. Stir in the curry leaves, mustard seeds, ginger and garlic.

In a small bowl, mix the turmeric, cumin, coriander and garam masala with 2 tablespoons of water to make a paste and stir this into the onion mixture. Pour the lentils into the pan, then pour in enough water to cover. Cook for 20 minutes on a gentle simmer. If the mixture thickens a lot, you may need to stir in another splash of water.

Meanwhile, place the chicken into a BBQ rack and top with the sliced lemon and bunches of herbs. Drizzle over the oil and season well. Place the rack on the BBQ and cook for 15 minutes, then turn and cook for a further 10 minutes. Alternatively, place in a roasting tin and roast in an oven preheated to 200°C (180°C fan)/400°F/gas 6 for 35–40 minutes.

Pile the chicken and charred lemons onto a large platter or board and sprinkle with the chopped herbs. Check the seasoning on the dhal, adding salt and pepper to taste, then spoon it into a bowl and pop alongside the chicken. Top the dhal with the remaining butter before serving.

PREVIOUS PAGE: YORKSHIRE DALES

Roast chicken with gnocchi

SERVES 6

1 large corn-fed chicken
  (about 1.6kg)
sea salt and freshly ground
  black pepper
25g salted butter

FOR THE GNOCCHI
4 large floury potatoes
75g '00' flour, plus extra for dusting
1 egg yolk
25g parmesan, grated,
  plus extra to serve
small bunch of flat-leaf parsley,
  chopped
small bunch of tarragon, chopped,
  plus extra to garnish
50g salted butter, for frying

Potatoes are, of course, the key to good gnocchi and I always use King Edward. Gnocchi are easy to make and you can even freeze them, then cook from frozen. This is a great combination with roast chicken, tarragon and parsley. Serve with a nice glass of English white wine and it doesn't get much better.

The night before you're going to cook this, brine the chicken. Put the chicken into a large deep bowl and cover with cold water. Add a small handful of salt to the water and pop the bowl in the fridge overnight.

Preheat the oven to 200°C (180°C fan)/400°F/gas 6.

Lift the chicken out of its soaking brine, pat dry with kitchen paper and put into a roasting tin. Smother in the butter, season well and roast for 1 hour. Prick the potato skins with the tip of a sharp knife and place in the oven to bake at the same time.

After an hour, remove the potatoes and set aside to cool a little. Check the chicken is cooked by piercing the thigh with a sharp knife. If the juices run clear, it's ready. If still pink, return to the oven and keep checking at 10-minute intervals. Once cooked, cover with foil and rest for 20 minutes.

When the potatoes are cool enough to handle, cut them in half, scoop out the flesh and put it through a potato ricer.

To make the gnocchi, mix the riced potato, flour, egg yolk, parmesan and herbs together in a large bowl. Season and mix again. Bring the mixture together with your hands to make a dough.

Roll out the dough on a lightly floured clean work surface into a sausage around 2cm thick, then cut the dough into 2-cm pieces.

Bring a large pan of salted water to the boil. Use a slotted spoon to carefully lower the gnocchi into the pan. Cook on a rolling boil and as soon as they float to the top, they're ready. Lift out with a slotted spoon to drain the water and set aside until all the gnocchi are cooked.

Heat the butter in a large frying pan. Once the butter has melted, fry the cooked gnocchi for 1–2 minutes until golden.

To serve, carve the chicken into portions and serve with the gnocchi, sprinkled with a few extra tarragon leaves and with some extra parmesan grated on top.

Chicken with morels

SERVES 2

50g salted butter

2 corn-fed chicken breasts,
French-trimmed (see tip)

sea salt and freshly ground
black pepper

100ml vin jaune du Jura wine
(or dry sherry, if unavailable)

600ml chicken stock

300ml double cream

200g morel mushrooms, cleaned

FOR THE CHARD

25g salted butter

small bunch of rainbow chard,
stalks and leaves roughly chopped

A classic dish cooked in the gardens of Belmond's Le Manoir Aux Quat'Saisons for one of the nicest friends I know, Raymond Blanc. Raymond started the place off as a tiny restaurant and grew it into one of the best, most beautiful restaurant hotels in the world and it is a reflection of his enthusiasm. The garden is a highlight and he showed me around the thousands of newly planted apple trees. This is one of his favourite dishes.

Heat three-quarters of the butter in a large non-stick pan over a medium heat. Once the butter is foaming, add the chicken to the pan, season, and fry for about 3–4 minutes on each side until golden. Lift the chicken onto a plate and set aside.

Drain the excess butter from the pan, then put the pan back over a medium heat and pour in the wine, chicken stock and cream. Bring the liquid to the boil, then add the mushrooms, season well, and simmer until the liquid has reduced by half. Stir in the remaining butter, then return the chicken to the pan to cook for 8–10 minutes. Taste to check the seasoning.

Meanwhile, cook the chard. Heat a medium saucepan over a medium heat and add the butter along with 50ml water. Bring to the boil, add the chard stalks and cook for 2 minutes. Add the chard leaves and cook for a further 1 minute, or until all the liquid has been absorbed. Season well.

Serve the chicken with the sauce and morel mushrooms spooned over the top, with the buttered chard alongside.

JAMES'S TIP

To French-trim a chicken, cut off the legs and set aside to use in another dish. Place a sharp knife onto the front end of the chicken and cut down either side of the wishbone. Discard the wishbone. Slice down either side of the breast bone and remove the chicken breasts, with the wings still attached. Trim the ends off the wings and discard. Run the knife around the end of each wing, push the meat down to reveal some of the bone and scrape the meat from the revealed bone.

Wild mushroom risotto with crispy chicken skin

SERVES 4

200g chicken skin

sea salt and freshly ground
  black pepper

2 whole onions, not peeled

500ml chicken stock

25g dried mushrooms

50g salted butter, plus extra
  as needed

2 garlic cloves, peeled and chopped

1 shallot, diced

200g risotto rice, such as Arborio

50ml dry white wine

200g wild mushrooms, brushed
  clean and torn if large

50g mascarpone

25g parmesan, grated

handful of micro herbs, to serve

This dish is a wonderful risotto with an exciting twist. Packed with flavour and simple to make, the chicken skin gives it an amazing texture and reminds me of the best pork scratchings ever. For me though, the real game-changer here is the umami... enjoy!

Preheat the oven to 200°C (180°C fan)/400°F/gas 6.

Lay the chicken skin flat on a baking sheet. Roast for 30–40 minutes until crisp. Drain on kitchen paper and season with a pinch of salt.

Place the whole onions in a deep pan, pour over the chicken stock and bring to the boil, then simmer for 30 minutes. Use a large metal spoon to scoop the onions onto a plate and leave to cool. Pop the dried mushrooms into the hot chicken stock and leave for 10–15 minutes to reconstitute.

Heat the butter in a deep non-stick pan over a medium heat. Once the butter is melted and foaming, add the garlic and shallot and cook for 2–3 minutes until starting to soften. Add the rice and stir until it is well coated in the butter. Stir in the wine and around three-quarters of the stock/mushroom mixture. Bring to the boil, then simmer for 15 minutes, stirring occasionally.

Meanwhile, dry fry the fresh mushrooms in a frying pan over a medium heat for 2–3 minutes until golden. Stir into the risotto towards the end of cooking.

Halve the poached onions through the root, then carefully lift into the mushroom frying pan. With the pan over a medium heat, char the onions, cut-side down, for 2 minutes until golden. Add a knob of butter to help them cook if you need to.

When the rice has finished cooking and is tender but still with a slight bite, stir in the remaining stock/mushroom mixture along with the mascarpone and parmesan, and season. The texture should be slightly runny at this stage.

Spoon the risotto among 4 warm bowls and top with the crispy chicken skin. Pull the onion layers apart from the root to make petals and dot over the top, then scatter over the micro herbs and serve.

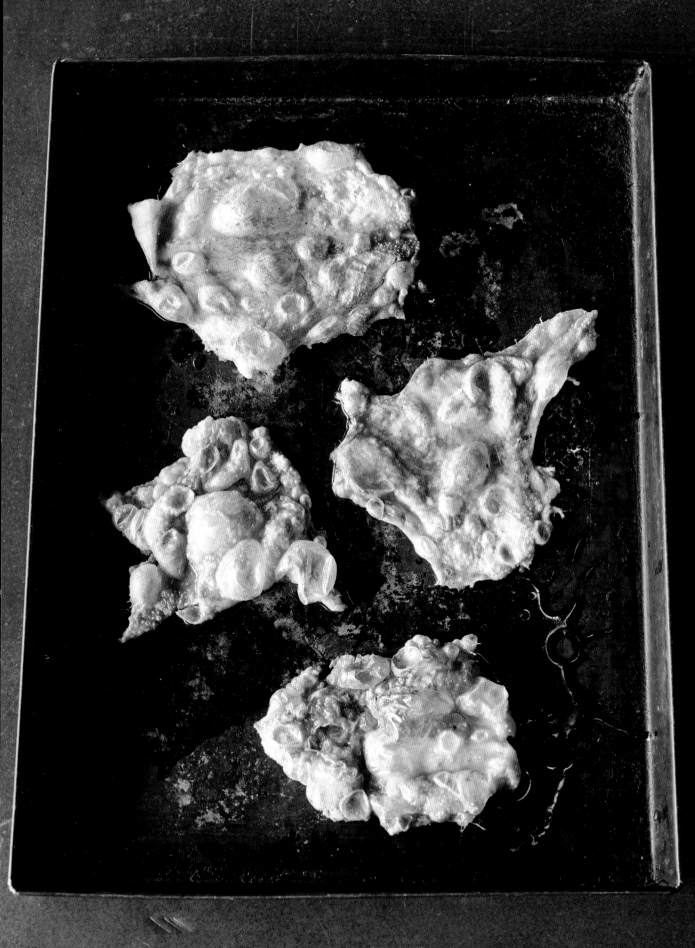

Hoisin duck on St Martin's Island

SERVES 2

2 large duck breasts (approx.
225g each), fillet removed

FOR THE HOISIN SAUCE
5 garlic cloves, sliced
2 red chillies, sliced
150g fermented black beans
(or canned black beans), puréed
200ml dark soy sauce
200ml veal jus
150ml rice wine vinegar
500g muscovado sugar
4 teaspoons sesame oil
1 teaspoon Chinese
five spice powder
sea salt and freshly ground
black pepper

TO SERVE
small bunch of purple
sprouting broccoli
bunch of spring onions, trimmed
bunch of asparagus
25ml olive oil
4 large mustard leaves
a few pak choi leaves

To be brutally honest, I got this idea from the great Gareth Ward in Wales. Making your own hoisin sauce is so simple and in a beautiful location like St Martin's in the Isles of Scilly it seemed the right thing to do, as well as put it together with the amazing local duck that is produced on the island. It is always surprising to see just how much produce a small collection of islands makes and produces. They even have their own gin distilleries – I know this because word got around and I was kindly given two bottles!

This recipe actually makes quite a large quantity of sauce. Any leftovers can be kept in the fridge in a sealed container for up to a week, or frozen for up to three months.

Light your BBQ. When the coals are silvery in colour, it's ready to cook on.

Put the duck on the BBQ, skin-side down, and cook for 3 minutes. Turn over and continue cooking for a further 3 minutes.

Meanwhile, put all the ingredients for the sauce into a medium saucepan, season well, and set on the BBQ rack next to the duck. Bring to the boil, stirring occasionally to help the sugar dissolve. Dip the duck breasts in the sauce, then set aside on a plate to rest.

Place the sprouting broccoli, spring onions and asparagus onto the BBQ, drizzle with the oil and cook for 2–3 minutes, turning halfway, until charred.

To serve, lay the mustard leaves on a platter and pile the pak choi and grilled vegetables on top. Slice the duck into finger-width strips, arrange on top, then drizzle with a little of the remaining sauce.

JAMES'S TIP
If you want a really smooth sauce, use a blender to whiz it up once it's cooked.

1920s duck and orange with duchess potatoes

SERVES 2

4 small duck breasts, fat scored
sea salt and freshly ground
  black pepper

FOR THE DUCHESS POTATOES
400g boiled potatoes, riced
pinch of nutmeg
3 egg yolks
2 tomatoes, peeled, deseeded
  and diced
½ shallot, diced
a few sprigs of tarragon
25g salted butter, melted

FOR THE SAUCE
1 orange
25ml brandy
25ml Cointreau (orange liqueur)
200ml veal jus
1 tablespoon salted butter

One of the most fun cooks of the series – trying to fit three reasonably sized middle-aged blokes in the kitchen of a moving train proved hilarious for my director and producer. This is a real classic that perfectly suited one of the best train journeys you can make in the UK on the Belmond Royal Scotsman. Chef Nick Nairn was in his element.

Preheat the oven to 200°C (180°C fan)/400°F/gas 6. Line a baking sheet with baking parchment.

Place the duck breasts, skin-side down, in a non-stick ovenproof frying pan over a medium heat. Cook for 3–4 minutes to render the fat and until the skin is golden. Season well, then turn the breasts over and transfer to the oven to cook for 4 minutes. Remove from the oven, transfer the duck breasts to a board and leave to rest for 6 minutes. Set the pan with the cooking juices aside.

Meanwhile, warm the potatoes in a pan, beat in the nutmeg along with some salt and pepper to season, then beat in the egg yolks. Spoon into a piping bag fitted with a star nozzle, then pipe 2 small nests, each with a hollow in the middle, onto the lined baking sheet. Divide the tomatoes, shallots and tarragon sprigs between the potato nests, spooning them into the middles, then brush the potato with the melted butter. Cook in the oven for 10 minutes, until golden and hot.

Next, make the sauce. Finely zest the orange, setting the zest aside. Peel, then segment the orange, cutting away any pith and reserving the juices. Drain the fat from the duck pan, keeping all the meat juices in the pan. Add the brandy and Cointreau, then flambé to burn off the alcohol, tipping the pan gently and carefully to ignite. When the flames have died down, stir in the orange zest then pour in the veal jus. Bring to the boil over a medium heat and simmer to reduce by half. Whisk in the butter, taste to check the seasoning, then pour in the reserved orange juice and segments and any resting juices from the duck.

To serve, slice the duck and divide between 2 plates. Pop a duchess potato alongside each and spoon over the sauce.

ROYAL SCOTSMAN, SCOTTISH HIGHLANDS

Partridge with black cherries and pommes Parisienne

SERVES 2

25g salted butter
2 tablespoons vegetable oil
2 partridges
a few sprigs of thyme
sea salt and freshly ground
  black pepper

FOR THE PURÉE
100ml store-bought black cherry
  purée, thawed if frozen
2 tablespoons xanthan gum

FOR THE POMMES PARISIENNE
around 300g fluffy potatoes,
  such as King Edward, peeled
25g salted butter
100g pearl or baby onions
a few sprigs of thyme
300ml beef stock

FOR THE SAUCE
100ml burgundy red wine
200ml beef jus
200g black cherries, stoned
25g salted butter

TO SERVE
50g mustard kale
25g salted butter

Most of the partridge you now see in the countryside or butchers is French red-leg partridge. Sadly the habitats for the UK's native grey-leg have thinned due to modern farming. That said, some areas are trying to recreate natural hedgerows for them to flourish once more. Online retailer Wild and Game is the best place to buy feathered game. The season runs from the first of September to the end of January.

Preheat the oven to 200°C (180°C fan)/400°F/gas 6.

Start with the purée. Place the cherry purée and xanthan gum into a blender and blitz for 1 minute until smooth. Spoon into a piping bag.

Heat the butter and oil in an ovenproof frying pan over a medium heat. Once the butter is melted and foaming, pop the partridges into the pan with the thyme and brown all over. Season well, then transfer to the oven for 10–12 minutes. Lift onto a tray lined with a clean J-cloth, cover and leave to rest. Set the pan aside to use for the kale.

To prepare the potatoes, use a melon baller to scoop out little balls of potato, trying to keep them as round as possible, and place in a bowl of water to cover. Just before cooking, drain and pat dry. Melt the butter in a separate frying pan over a medium heat, add the potatoes, the pearl or baby onions and the thyme, and cook until the potatoes and onions are golden. Pour in the stock and bring to the boil, then simmer until all the liquid has been absorbed. Season well.

In the partridge pan, fry the kale with the butter over a medium heat for around 1 minute, just until the leaves wilt. Spoon onto the tray with the partridge. Place the pan back on the hob.

To make the sauce, pour the wine into the kale pan and bring to the boil. Simmer to reduce the liquid by half, then pour in the jus and continue to simmer until reduced by half again. Stir in the fresh cherries and the butter and season well.

Put the partridge on a board and use a sharp knife to carve off the legs and the breast from each. Divide the kale between 2 serving plates, place the partridge alongside and add a spoonful of the pommes Parisienne mixture. Dot with cherry purée and spoon over the sauce, then serve.

Grouse pithivier with bramble purée

SERVES 2

FOR THE PITHIVIER
2 large Savoy cabbage leaves,
   tough stems removed
a little vegetable oil, for greasing
4 grouse breasts, diced
100g coarse pâté of your choice
sea salt and freshly ground
   black pepper
200g ready-rolled all-butter pastry
1 egg, beaten

FOR THE PURÉE
100g brambles/blackberries
1 tablespoon xanthan gum

FOR THE SAUCE
300ml chicken stock
1 tablespoon salted butter

I really wanted to include game in this book and series because I love the whole ethos behind it so much – it's pure, honest food. Grouse has to be the king of all game birds, available from the glorious twelfth of August and throughout the Christmas period. It can be cooked in so many different ways, but this is one of my favourites. At first glance it looks fiddly but it's actually very simple to prepare and cook. As with all game, don't overcook it.

Preheat the oven to 180°C (160°C fan)/350°F/gas 4. Line a baking sheet with baking parchment.

Bring a medium saucepan of water to the boil and add a pinch of salt. Blanch the cabbage leaves for 1 minute then drain and pat dry with kitchen paper.

Oil 2 teacups and line each with clingfilm, then line each with a cabbage leaf. Layer up the grouse meat and pâté in alternate layers in the cups, seasoning each layer. Fold the cabbage over the top to form parcels.

Unroll the pastry on a board, then use a 12-cm round cutter to stamp out 2 circles from the pastry. Use a 16-cm round cutter to stamp out 2 more. Place the smaller circles onto the lined baking sheet and top with the cabbage parcels, then cover each dome with the larger pastry circles. Press down to secure the edges – you can use the smaller cutter to do this, which will both seal the pastry edges together and neaten it. Brush all over with the beaten egg, then bake for 18–20 minutes. Remove from the oven and let rest for 3–4 minutes.

While the pies are baking, make the sauce. Pour the stock into a small pan and add the butter. Bring to the boil, then simmer until reduced by half and season well.

To make the purée, put the brambles/blackberries in a pan with 1 tablespoon of water. Bring to the boil over a medium heat, then add the xanthan gum and whiz with a hand-held stick blender to make a purée. Spoon into a squeezy bottle or a piping bag.

To serve, snip the end of the piping bag, if using, and pipe a small circle of bramble purée onto your serving plates. Cut each pithivier in half and sit either side of the purée, then spoon over the sauce.

MEAT

Veal with pan-fried apples, black pudding fritters and mustard sauce

SERVES 2

400g veal steak, about 5cm thick
sea salt and freshly ground
  black pepper
100g salted butter
a few sprigs of thyme

FOR THE MUSTARD SAUCE
25g salted butter
½ shallot, diced
1 garlic clove, finely chopped
25ml Irish whiskey
2 tablespoons grainy mustard
½ teaspoon English mustard
200ml veal jus
75ml double cream

FOR THE FRITTERS
vegetable oil, for frying
50g plain flour
2 eggs, beaten
50g panko breadcrumbs
200g black pudding,
  sliced into 1-cm rounds

FOR THE PAN-FRIED APPLES
15g salted butter
2 apples, cored and sliced into
  1-cm rounds

FOR THE MASH
200g cooked potatoes, riced
50g salted butter
50ml double cream

We now produce so much good veal in this country that we ought to eat more of it rather than importing it from Holland or elsewhere. In terms of ethics, many farmers will agree with me that consuming veal is no worse than drinking milk, so do give it a try. Treat it like steak and it can take strong flavours, as here.

Preheat the oven to 200°C (180°C fan)/400°F/gas 6.

Put the veal on a board and season all over. Melt the butter in a large ovenproof frying pan over a medium-high heat. Once melted, pan-fry the veal with the thyme sprigs for 2 minutes. Transfer the pan to the oven and cook for a further 6 minutes. Transfer the veal to a warm plate, cover and leave to rest. Return the pan to the heat.

To make the sauce, heat the butter in the veal frying pan and stir in the shallot and garlic. Season and cook quickly over a medium-high heat for 2 minutes then pour in the whiskey and stir in both types of mustard. Pour in the veal jus and cream and bring to the boil, then simmer until reduced by half and season again.

Heat the vegetable oil in a deep-fat fryer to 180°C/350°F or in a deep heavy-based saucepan until a breadcrumb sizzles and turns brown when dropped into it. (Note: hot oil can be dangerous; do not leave unattended.) Line a large plate with kitchen paper.

Put the flour into a shallow dish, the eggs into a separate shallow dish and the breadcrumbs into another. Season the flour. Coat the black pudding first in the flour, then dip into the beaten egg, then cover with the breadcrumbs. Carefully lower into the hot oil and deep-fry until golden and crispy. Lift out with a slotted spoon to drain on the kitchen paper and season with salt.

Heat the butter for the apples in a frying pan and pan-fry the apple slices on each side until golden and soft. Season with a pinch of salt.

For the mash, put the riced potatoes into a medium pan and add the butter and cream. Place the pan over a medium heat, season well and beat everything together, then transfer the mash to a piping bag.

To serve, slice the veal in half and place each piece onto a warmed plate. Pipe a rosette of mash alongside and layer up a stack of the apples and black pudding fritters, then spoon over the sauce.

Steak with mushrooms, three ways

SERVES 3

1 tablespoon olive oil

3 x 200-g sirloin steaks

sea salt and freshly ground
  black pepper

1 tablespoon ketjap/kecap manis

FOR THE MUSHROOM KETCHUP

250g shiitake mushrooms

150ml rice wine vinegar

7g agar agar

FOR THE GRILLED MUSHROOMS

6 large flat mushrooms

1 tablespoon olive oil

FOR THE MUSHROOM PICKLE

100ml rice wine vinegar

25g caster sugar

1 teaspoon sea salt

100g wild mushrooms

The quality of the mushrooms that can be farmed in places all around the UK is amazing. This spot – Forest Fungi – in Devon is no exception, as the mushrooms seem to be grown in what looks like a bungalow which has been kitted out into a high-tech mushroom farm. The stuff they are producing there is brilliant.

First, make the mushroom ketchup. Put the shiitake mushrooms in a medium saucepan along with 350ml water and bring to the boil. Strain out the mushrooms, reserving the cooking stock. Return the cooking stock to the pan, add the vinegar and bring to the boil again, then whisk in the agar agar. Transfer to a bowl and put in the fridge to set. Once the mixture has set, blitz in a food processor, then spoon into a piping bag and set aside.

Light your BBQ. When the coals are silvery in colour, it's ready to cook on. Alternatively, heat a griddle pan over a medium heat until hot.

Rub the oil over each side of the steaks and season well. Lay the steaks on the BBQ or griddle pan and cook for 4 minutes, then flip over and cook for a further 4 minutes. Brush with the ketjap manis, then set aside to rest on a plate.

Put the large flat mushrooms onto the BBQ or griddle pan, drizzle with oil and cook for 2–3 minutes until charred on both sides.

To make the pickle, place the vinegar, sugar and salt in a pan and bring to the boil, stirring to dissolve the sugar and salt. Add the wild mushrooms to the pickle mixture, then remove from the heat and stir everything together.

To serve, pile the grilled mushrooms onto a large platter and spoon the pickled mushrooms over the top. Cut the steak into thick slices and sit the pieces on top. Snip off the end of the piping bag of mushroom ketchup and pipe it all over the steak.

DEVON

Beef and beer stew with dumplings

SERVES 6

2 tablespoons plain flour
sea salt and freshly ground
   black pepper
2kg rump steak, cut into 6-cm cubes
2 tablespoons olive oil
3 tablespoons salted butter
1 onion, diced
2 large carrots, each cut
   into 4 chunks
2 sticks of celery, diced
1 tablespoon Worcestershire sauce
500ml beer
300ml beef stock

FOR THE DUMPLINGS
125g beef suet
200g self-raising flour
small bunch of flat-leaf parsley,
   chopped
1 tablespoon salt

Wherever you live in the UK, you will always be able to get great beef and great beer thanks to the amazing pasture, barley and wheat that this country produces – so it's no surprise that this dish is a staple all over the British Isles. It really had to be in the book.

Tip the flour into a large bowl and season well. Add the beef and toss to coat in the flour.

Heat 1 tablespoon of the oil and 1 tablespoon of the butter in a large lidded ovenproof pan or casserole over a medium heat and brown the beef in 2 batches, adding the remaining oil and another tablespoon of butter as needed. Return all the browned beef to the pan, then add the onion, carrots, celery, Worcestershire sauce, beer and stock and season well. Cover with the lid and bring to the boil, then reduce the heat and simmer for 1½ hours until the beef is tender and can easily be pulled apart with forks. Check the seasoning and stir in the remaining tablespoon of butter.

To make the dumplings, mix all the ingredients together in a large bowl, then pour over 150ml cold water and use a knife to stir the mixture together to make a rough dough. Place spoonfuls of the mixture on top of the stew to make individual dumplings, then replace the lid and continue to cook for 20 minutes.

To serve, spoon the stew into warmed bowls and top with the dumplings.

Wagyu beef with parsley-crusted bone marrow and red wine sauce

SERVES 2

**FOR THE PARSLEY-CRUSTED
BONE MARROW**
4 x 10-cm cut bone marrow,
   pre-soaked in well-salted water
   in the fridge for 24 hours
2 teaspoons Dijon mustard
2 pickled onions, finely diced
2 teaspoons finely chopped
   flat-leaf parsley

FOR THE SAUCE
15g salted butter
2 shallots, diced
2 garlic cloves, crushed
100ml red wine
300ml veal jus
1 tablespoon Dijon mustard
1 teaspoon Worcestershire sauce
1 teaspoon sherry vinegar
sea salt and freshly ground
   black pepper

FOR THE WAGYU BEEF
2 x 300-g Wagyu beef, Denver cut
15g salted butter
2 tablespoons vegetable oil

TO SERVE
large handful of watercress

When Gareth Ward tells you some of the best beef in the world can be found in Wales and it's Wagyu and it's just down the road from his place Ynyshir, famed for its meat dishes, then you pay attention... He wasn't wrong!

Roast bone marrow is another ingredient we don't cook enough with – it's simple to prepare and cook and it tastes fantastic. Here, you need to start preparing it the day before.

The Denver cut of steak is from the chuck part of the cow.

Preheat the oven to 230°C (210°C fan)/450°F/gas 8.

Drain the soaked bone marrow and pat dry, then place upright in a roasting tin, season well, and roast for 40 minutes. At this point, remove the tin from the oven and take out 2 bone marrow and set aside to cool a little. When cool enough to handle, pop the marrow out of the bones into a bowl by pushing a thin butter knife through from one end. Discard the bones and set the marrow aside.

Top the remaining 2 bone marrow in the roasting tin with 1 teaspoon each of the mustard and sprinkle the diced pickled onions and parsley on top. Turn the oven down to 180°C (160°C fan)/350°F/gas 4 and roast the marrow for a further 10 minutes.

Meanwhile, make the sauce. Melt the butter in a saucepan over a medium heat, then stir in the shallots and garlic. Season well and cook for around 2 minutes until just softened. Pour in the wine and bring to the boil, then add the veal jus. Bring to a simmer and cook until the sauce has reduced by half, stirring every now and then. Stir in the mustard, Worcestershire sauce, sherry vinegar and the reserved marrow, season and stir well until you have a smooth sauce.

Heat a large non-stick frying pan over a medium-high heat until hot. Season the steaks all over, then add the butter and oil to the pan. Once the butter has stopped foaming, add the steaks and cook for 2 minutes on one side, then flip them over and cook for a further 2 minutes. Lift onto a board to rest for 5 minutes.

To serve, sit each parsley-crusted bone marrow on a plate and lay the steaks alongside. Spoon over the sauce and garnish with watercress.

WELSH WAGYU CATTLE, WALES

Steamed beef puddings with black garlic and pea purées

SERVES 4

FOR THE FILLING
25g salted butter,
  plus extra for greasing
1 shallot, diced
1 garlic clove, crushed
1 carrot, diced
250g ox cheek, diced
350g beef mince
a few sprigs of thyme, leaves picked
sea salt and freshly ground
  black pepper
250ml red wine
500ml beef stock

FOR THE PASTRY
250g plain flour,
  plus extra for dusting
125g shredded suet
pinch of salt

FOR THE BLACK GARLIC PURÉE
50g black garlic cloves, peeled
75ml beef stock

FOR THE PEA PURÉE
200g frozen peas
75ml beef stock

FOR THE SAUCE
300ml beef jus
a knob of salted butter

TO SERVE
4 cornichons, diced

Steamed pudding and beef stew with peas… what's not to like? My chefs came up with the cornichon garnish to cut through the fat of the suet and it works. This is a great dinner party dish and it's one that I now do in the restaurant.

Melt the butter in a large non-stick casserole with a lid over a medium heat. Stir in the shallot, garlic and carrot and cook for 2–3 minutes until softened. Add the ox cheek and mince and cook for around 5 minutes until browned. Add the thyme, season well, then pour in the wine and stock. Bring to the boil, then reduce the heat to low, cover and leave to braise for 1½ hours until the meat is tender. Stir occasionally and add a splash of boiling water if it looks dry. Set aside to cool.

To make the pastry, mix the flour, suet and salt in a large bowl. Add 150–175ml water and stir together to a sticky dough. Bring the mixture together with your hands, then tip onto a lightly floured clean work surface. Dust the dough lightly with flour and roll out to 3mm thick.

Grease 4 x 8-cm dariole moulds with butter. Stamp out 4 rounds of pastry using the top of the moulds, then divide the remaining dough into 4 and use each piece to line the moulds. Fill each with an equal portion of the filling mixture. Brush the edges of the pastry with water, top with the pastry circles and seal the edges, trimming any excess.

Cover the top of the puddings with 2 layers of greaseproof paper, then cover with foil and secure with string. Steam the puddings in a steamer, or on an upturned plate in a large saucepan half-filled with water and covered with a lid, for 20 minutes.

To make the purées, combine the garlic and stock in a small pan, bring to the boil, then simmer for 2 minutes. Meanwhile, combine the peas, stock and 1 tablespoon of water in a separate saucepan, bring to the boil and cook for 1 minute. Use a handheld stick blender to blitz each until smooth, then spoon into piping bags or squeezy bottles.

For the sauce, pour the beef jus into a small pan and bring to the boil, then simmer until reduced by half. Whisk in the butter and season.

To serve, unwrap the puddings and upturn each into the centre of a plate. Spoon the sauce around and dot with alternate purées. Arrange the cornichons on top of each pudding and spoon over more sauce.

Steak with whisky-braised onions and mustard sauce

SERVES 2

4 onions, peeled
50ml whisky
600ml beef stock
100g salted butter
1 garlic clove, crushed
a few pine sprigs, washed
    and patted dry
1–2 tablespoons olive oil
sea salt and freshly ground
    black pepper
400g rump steak, 5cm thick
150g long-stem broccoli

FOR THE SAUCE
2 tablespoons Scottish
    grainy mustard
½ teaspoon English mustard
2 tablespoons salted butter
25ml whisky
75ml double cream

Every chef becomes obsessed with certain ingredients at some point in the year and right now, my obsession is onions. These, combined with steak and a simple mustard sauce, were a favourite dish of Johnny on Camera Two when we were filming the show.

If using, light your BBQ. When the coals are silvery in colour, it's ready to cook on.

Place the whole onions in a pan with the whisky and beef stock. Cover and bring to the boil then reduce the heat slightly and simmer for 40 minutes. Use a slotted spoon to lift the onions out of their cooking liquor and set aside to cool a little. Reserve the liquor.

Meanwhile, place the butter, garlic and pine sprigs into a separate pan and place over a low heat to melt the butter.

If not cooking on the BBQ, preheat a griddle pan over a high heat. Cut the onions in half horizontally, then drizzle over the oil and season well. Cook on the griddle pan or on the BBQ, flat-side down, for a couple of minutes until charred. Lift onto a plate and set aside.

Season the steak all over, then brush with some of the melted pine butter. Cook on the hot griddle pan or on the BBQ for 2 minutes, then brush with more butter, flip over and cook for another 2 minutes.

Add the long-stem broccoli to the pan or BBQ for the last 2 minutes of cooking, again brushing with pine butter. Lift the steak onto a board and rest for 4 minutes.

To make the sauce, put both types of mustard in a pan with 1 tablespoon of the butter and 200ml of the reserved onion cooking liquor. Pour in the whisky, then flambé to burn off the alcohol, tipping the pan gently and carefully to ignite. Place over a medium heat and simmer until the liquid has reduced by half, then stir in the cream and season well. Whisk in the remaining 1 tablespoon of butter to finish.

Slice the steak into 3-cm thick slices and place on a platter with the broccoli, then spoon over the sauce. Pull the onions into petals and dot around before serving.

Skye lobster and steak with haggis butter

SERVES 6

2 x 200-g fillet steaks

sea salt and freshly ground
  black pepper

1–2 tablespoons olive oil

½ beef Oxo stock cube, crumbled

large bunch of fresh seaweed,
  well washed

3 lobsters, cut in half lengthways

6 langoustines

1 lemon, cut into 4 wedges

FOR THE HAGGIS BUTTER

500g softened salted butter

400g haggis, crumbled

1 shallot, diced

small bunch of flat-leaf parsley,
  chopped, plus extra sprigs
  to garnish

Skye was the TV crew's favourite place to visit on the entire trip. Relatively easy to get to, thanks to the bridge, it's a mecca for tourists who love wildlife and countryside views like no other. This is what happened to my mate Paul Rankin – he fell in love with the place and has just bought Skye's oldest pub, The Stein Inn, right on the shore of the Waternish peninsula.

A stone's throw away is Loch Bay restaurant. Armed with a Michelin star, this tiny restaurant is run by husband and wife, Michael and Laurence Smith; together they have turned this small village into the Padstow of Scotland. Their food is made from ingredients that are – literally – on their doorstep, like lobster and langoustine. Go to Skye for the views – and for Loch Bay's brilliant food!

Place a griddle pan over a medium heat and heat until hot. Alternatively, light your BBQ. When the coals are silvery in colour, it's ready to cook on.

Season the steaks and drizzle a little oil over each side. Place on the griddle pan or BBQ rack and cook for 2–3 minutes. Sprinkle the crumbled stock cube over the uncooked side, then flip over and cook for a further 2 minutes.

While the steaks are cooking, mix the butter, haggis, shallot and chopped parsley together in a bowl, seasoning as you go, until combined.

Transfer the steaks to a board, dot a tablespoon of the haggis butter onto each one and set aside to rest.

Place a large, shallow paella-style pan over a medium heat or onto the BBQ. Pile in the seaweed, then pour in 500ml water. Place the lobster halves on top, cut-side up, smother in the haggis butter and scatter over the parsley sprigs. Cover the pan tightly with foil and let it steam bake for 7 minutes, then peel back the foil, add the langoustines to the pan, replace the foil and cook for a further 3 minutes.

To serve, remove the foil, slice the steak and add to the lobster pan, then garnish with the lemon wedges to squeeze over.

Stuffed porchetta

SERVES 10

3kg boned pork middle loin,
  skin scored

FOR THE STUFFING
300g Dorset Blue Vinny cheese,
  crumbled
1 medium onion, grated
2 English apples, grated
½ teaspoon ground cinnamon
2 tablespoons fennel seeds
100g sultanas
100g walnuts, roughly chopped
small bunch of parsley, chopped
50g breadcrumbs
2 eggs, beaten
sea salt and freshly ground
  black pepper

TO SERVE
chutneys and pickles
watercress (optional)

Dorset Blue Vinny from Woodbridge Farm, Dorset, is one of Paul Ainsworth's favourite cheeses, and he bought masses during filming. I went to Purbeck on his advice to visit one of the best pork producers I've ever found in the south. There I saw the famous hairy Mangalitza pigs, which translates as 'pig of lard'. This dish combines that cheese and pork and it tastes so good.

Preheat the oven to 240°C (220°C fan)/475°F/gas 9.

Put all the ingredients for the stuffing in a large bowl, seasoning well at the end. Mix until all the ingredients are thoroughly combined.

Lay the pork on a board and unroll it skin-side down. Using a sharp knife and starting at one end, carefully cut the meat in half horizontally, working almost to the very end so that it's still attached on one side. Open out the length of the meat so that you have a very long rectangle. Spoon the stuffing over the entire surface of the meat and smooth over so that it sits in an even layer. Starting from the end with no skin attached, roll the meat up tightly along its length to enclose the filling. Secure with string: cut a length of string at least 5 times the length of the joint. Make a noose in the end of the string, loop it around the pork, then pull the string through the noose and pull it tight. Continue to work down the joint, wrapping the string around the underside of the joint and back around to meet the string at the top, then feeding the string over and under the string at the top, pulling it taught each time. Tie it at the end to secure.

Place the stuffed pork onto a rack set in a roasting tray and roast for 30 minutes. After this time, turn the oven down to 140°C (120°C fan)/ 275°F/gas 1 and roast for another 1½ hours. Remove from the oven and let cool. Transfer to a large plate and chill in the fridge overnight.

When you're ready to serve, take the porchetta out of the fridge and leave for 30 minutes to come to room temperature. Cut off the string, then slice and serve with chutneys and pickles, and a handful of watercress, if you like.

SANDBANKS, DORSET

BBQ pork and chicken meat feast with apple and celeriac slaw

SERVES 4–6

4 large pork chops
  (ideally Mangalitza pork)
6 merguez sausages
4 x 150-g skinless chicken breasts
sea salt and freshly ground
  black pepper
2 Cox's apples, thinly sliced
150g 'nduja sausage,
  torn into small pieces
1 tablespoon vegetable oil
2 small black pudding rings
4 picante chorizo sausages
6 tablespoons maple syrup

FOR THE SLAW
3 egg yolks
1 tablespoon Dijon mustard
200ml vegetable oil
1 celeriac, peeled
4 Cox's apples
2 tablespoons wholegrain mustard

When you have talent on your journey like Paul Ainsworth you have to put it to good use, so while he cooked all the meat on the beach on one of the islands in Poole harbour, I made this simple little slaw that goes well with all grilled meats, or tastes good just on its own.

Light your BBQ. When the coals are silvery in colour, it's ready to cook on.

Put the pork chops onto the BBQ, along with the merguez sausages and cook for about 15–20 minutes, turning regularly.

Carefully pull away the small fillets from the chicken breasts, then use a sharp knife to cut horizontally through the length of each breast, almost to the other side, to create a pocket in each one. Season, then push a quarter of the sliced apples into each pocket along with the pieces of 'nduja, then push the small fillets back into the breasts to plug the holes. Brush the chicken all over with the oil, then place the chicken onto the BBQ and cook for 15 minutes, turning halfway.

Add the black pudding and chorizo sausages to the BBQ and cook for 2–3 minutes on each side, turning them as necessary.

Meanwhile, whisk the egg yolks and Dijon mustard together in a medium bowl until smooth. Slowly pour the vegetable oil into the bowl, starting with a little drizzle and whisking well. This is easiest to do with an electric hand whisk. Continue to drizzle in the remaining oil, whisking all the time, until the mixture has thickened into a mayonnaise. Season to taste and set aside.

Cut the celeriac into thin slices, around 3mm thick, then slice each piece into thin batons. Repeat with the apples. To assemble the slaw, stir the wholegrain mustard into the mayonnaise to make a rémoulade, then add the celeriac and apple batons and stir to combine.

Finally, drizzle the maple syrup over the pork chops and cook for a further couple of minutes.

Transfer all the meat to a large warm serving platter and serve with the slaw on the side.

MANGALITZA PIGS, ARNE, DORSET

Pork and chorizo skewers with a fricassee of Yorkshire vegetables

SERVES 4

2 x 400-g pork fillets, sliced
  into 5-cm cubes
200g chorizo, cut into
  2-cm thick pieces
1–2 tablespoons olive oil
sea salt and freshly ground
  black pepper

FOR THE FRICASSEE
50g salted butter
6 asparagus spears,
  halved widthways
6 baby leeks, halved widthways
50g soft chorizo (such as
  sobrasada), sliced
100g podded fresh peas
  (prepared weight)
100g podded and skinned
  broad beans (prepared weight
  from 400g)
3 baby courgettes, thinly sliced
6 wild garlic leaves, washed
  (or fresh chives if unavailable)
small bunch of flat-leaf parsley,
  chopped

TO SERVE
a few wild garlic flowers (optional)

This dish used the Yorkshire pork chorizo that Brian Turner found for me and we cooked it overlooking the Peak District, a stone's throw from Coniston Country Estate near Skipton. I want to thank the gamekeeper and his team for building a windbreak of bits of wood, tarpaulin and Land Rovers to allow this cook to happen. It tasted great though!

Light your BBQ. When the coals are silvery in colour, it's ready to cook on. If using bamboo skewers, soak them in water before cooking.

Push the pork and chorizo pieces alternately onto 8 skewers, dividing them equally. Drizzle with the oil and season all over. Place onto the BBQ and cook for 7–8 minutes, turning occasionally until golden and just charred.

Heat a saucepan over a medium heat or on the BBQ until hot, then add the butter and 50ml water. When the mixture is melted and bubbling, add the asparagus and leeks, season well and cook for 2 minutes. Stir the soft chorizo through the mixture, then add the peas, broad beans and courgettes and cook for a further 2 minutes. Finally, stir through the wild garlic leaves and parsley and taste to check the seasoning.

To serve, spoon the vegetables onto a large warmed platter, place the skewers on top and scatter over the wild garlic flowers (if using).

Port Erin TT pork burgers

SERVES 4

FOR THE BURGERS
1kg pork mince
1 egg yolk
50g fresh breadcrumbs
sea salt and freshly ground
  black pepper
1–2 tablespoons olive oil

FOR THE SAUCE
2 Cox's apples, diced
1 Bramley apple, diced
2 tablespoons gochujang chilli paste

FOR THE SALAD
1 red onion, finely sliced
2 sticks of celery, thinly sliced
small bunch of flat-leaf parsley,
  chopped
1 green chilli, diced
1 little gem lettuce, sliced
2 tablespoons mayonnaise
juice of 1 lemon

TO SERVE
4 brioche buns, halved through
  the middle
1–2 tablespoons olive oil
a few walnuts, chopped
4 long cocktail sticks

I made this dish for TT week on the Isle of Man and it didn't let me down as, when we set up the cook by the harbour, in less than two minutes we were joined by bikers killing time, dodging the fog and rain showers during TT week. A whole family descended on us to enjoy these, packed full of flavour. Try not to make them too thick, as the fat from the pork can cause the burgers to burn, but equally don't overcook them!

Light your BBQ. When the coals are silvery in colour, it's ready to cook on. Alternatively, heat a large flat griddle pan over a medium heat until hot.

Start by making the sauce. Set a flameproof non-stick saucepan on the BBQ or over a medium heat. When hot, add the apples, gochujang paste and 2 tablespoons of water and bring to the boil, then simmer for 2–3 minutes. Remove from the heat and set aside.

For the burgers, mix the pork, egg yolk, breadcrumbs and plenty of seasoning together in a large bowl. Roughly divide the mixture into 4 pieces, then shape each into a large burger and drizzle a little oil over each one. Place onto the BBQ or the hot griddle pan and cook for 4 minutes, then flip over and cook for a further 4 minutes.

Mix all the ingredients for the salad together in a large bowl and season well.

To serve, drizzle the cut-side of each brioche bun with a little oil and toast on the BBQ or griddle pan, cut-side down, until lightly toasted. Spoon a little sauce onto the bottom of each brioche bun, place a burger on top and sprinkle with the chopped walnuts. Pile on the salad, pop the bun tops on and secure each with a cocktail stick.

Lamb chops with olive glaze and hispi cabbage

SERVES 4–6

12 lamb chops
sea salt and freshly ground
   black pepper
1 hispi cabbage,
   quartered lengthways
1–2 tablespoons olive oil
juice of ½ lemon
bunch of chives, chopped

FOR THE OLIVE GLAZE
100g caster sugar
3 star anise
200g black olives, stoned

TO SERVE
100ml natural yogurt
12 slices air-dried ham
1–2 tablespoons extra virgin olive oil

The best part of this was seeing TT legend John McGuinness 20 yards away watching me cover his favourite dish of lamb chops with one of his least favourite ingredients – olives – whilst cooking this in the paddock at the TT. Despite his fears, the mechanics and I agreed that it did work and made the lamb chops super tasty as well as the cabbage. I did text him in advance to find out what he wanted me to cook, but pie and chips is quite difficult on a disposable BBQ!

Light your BBQ. When the coals are silvery in colour, it's ready to cook on. Alternatively, heat a large griddle pan over a medium heat until hot.

First, make the glaze. Put the sugar and the star anise into a pan along with 50ml water. Bring to the boil over a medium heat, then remove from the heat and leave to cool. Take out and discard the star anise, then transfer to a food processor along with the olives. Blitz until smooth, then pass through a sieve into a bowl and set aside.

Season the chops with salt and pepper, then place onto the BBQ or griddle pan and cook for 4 minutes on each side. Transfer to a board to rest.

Bring a large pan of water to the boil, then add the cabbage quarters and blanch for 2–3 minutes. Drain well, then drizzle over the oil and season well. Place the cabbage quarters, flat-side down, onto the BBQ or griddle pan and cook for 2–3 minutes on each flat side, turning once, until nicely charred. Lift onto a large platter, squeeze over the lemon juice, sprinkle with the chives and season again.

Brush the rested lamb chops all over with the olive glaze, then pile them onto the platter alongside the cabbage. Spoon the yogurt over the top, arrange the ham around the platter, then finally drizzle over the extra virgin olive oil before serving.

Blackface lamb steaks with ratatouille and salsa verde

SERVES 4

small bunch of heather
4 x 200-g lamb steaks
sea salt and freshly ground
  black pepper

FOR THE RATATOUILLE
50ml olive oil
1 onion, diced
2 garlic cloves, crushed
1 courgette, diced
½ aubergine, diced
1 red pepper diced
4 tomatoes, diced
small bunch of basil, torn

FOR THE SALSA VERDE
small bunch of mint,
  leaves picked and chopped
1 garlic clove, crushed
2 tablespoons nonpareille capers
small bunch of flat-leaf parsley,
  chopped
4 anchovies, chopped
zest and juice of 1 lemon
50ml olive oil

Scottish blackface sheep are one of the most common domestic sheep in the UK. Found in some of the most exposed locations, like the Highlands and Dartmoor, they are believed to have originated from Scotland as early as 1503. There are different varieties of blackface lamb that can be found all over the world and particularly America. It is prized not just for its meat, but also for its wool.

Light your BBQ. When the coals are silvery in colour, it's ready to cook on.

Scatter the heather over the coals, then place the rack onto the BBQ. Place the lamb onto the rack and cook for 2–3 minutes on each side, seasoning as you go. Lift onto a board and let rest.

To make the ratatouille, heat a flameproof pan on the BBQ until hot then add the oil and stir in the onions and garlic. After 1 minute, add the diced courgette, then after another minute, stir in the diced aubergine. Cook for a further 1 minute, then stir in the pepper, followed by the tomatoes and basil. Season, then gently simmer for a further 2 minutes.

To make the salsa verde, mix all the ingredients together in a bowl and season well.

To serve, spoon the ratatouille into a bowl. Place the lamb onto 4 dinner plates and spoon over the salsa verde. Drizzle over a little more olive oil if you'd like to, and let everyone help themselves to the ratatouille.

Welsh lamb ragout with penne

SERVES 6–8

25g salted butter

3 garlic cloves, chopped

1 onion, diced

2 carrots, diced

1 leek, diced

1 celery stick, diced

300g lamb mince

200g lamb leg, diced into
  1-cm cubes

1 tablespoon tomato purée

sea salt and freshly ground
  black pepper

500ml lamb or beef stock

100ml red wine

200g canned chopped tomatoes

2 bay leaves

400g fresh penne pasta

large bunch of basil leaves,
  roughly torn

50g parmesan

I genuinely meant it when I said during our filming in the Brecon Beacons that it's tempting not to bother going abroad on holiday when we have places like this on our doorstep. The scenery around Wales is spectacular, it was one of my favourite locations on the whole trip, and I loved it so much that I have been back there four times since filming.

Heat the butter in a large non-stick saucepan over a medium heat. Once the butter is foaming, stir in the garlic, onion, carrots, leek and celery and cook gently for around 5 minutes until starting to soften. Increase the heat to high, then add all the lamb and cook for 2–3 minutes, stirring everything together and using a wooden spoon to break down the mince. Stir in the tomato purée, season well, then pour in the stock, wine and chopped tomatoes. Give everything a good stir, then tuck the bay leaves into the mixture. Leave to bubble over a high heat for 20–25 minutes, stirring occasionally, until it reduces by around half.

Bring a large saucepan of water to the boil, add a good pinch of salt, then add the pasta and cook for 2 minutes. Use a slotted spoon to lift the pasta out of the pan and transfer it to the pan with the sauce. Cook for a further 2 minutes, then stir in the basil and season.

Divide between pasta bowls, then grate over the parmesan and serve.

Rump of lamb with vegetables in a garlic and seaweed butter

SERVES 2

FOR THE LAMB

1 tablespoon vegetable oil

15g salted butter

a sprig of rosemary

2 x 200-g lamb rumps

sea salt and freshly ground
  black pepper

FOR THE MASH

200g cooked potatoes, riced

50ml double cream

100g salted butter

**FOR THE GARLIC AND
SEAWEED BUTTER**

1 small garlic clove, crushed

½ shallot, diced

50g salted butter, softened

½ teaspoon dried dulse seaweed

FOR THE VEGETABLES

6 asparagus, halved

100g peas

75g podded and skinned
  broad beans (prepared weight
  from 225g)

100g green beans, topped,
  tailed and halved

a few sprigs of chives, chopped

You can use any seaweed for this, fresh or dried, but of course I urge you to buy it from the UK. Dulse, kelp and other types can easily be found online and when simply cooked with broad beans and peas like this, they act as a great seasoning.

The seaweed around the British Isles is amazing but the stuff from Rathlin Island is, for me, the best of the bunch. Rathlin has a rich history of harvesting it and old drying kilns can be seen all around the small island. Around 125 people live here and one of the best things I remember about it (I do not have fond memories of the rough crossing) was the tiny – and I mean tiny – GP surgery where, as the locals took great pleasure in telling me, Richard Branson was taken when he crashed his balloon!

Preheat the oven to 200°C (180°C fan)/400°F/gas 6.

For the lamb, heat the oil and butter in a large ovenproof frying pan over a medium heat. Once melted, add the rosemary sprig and lamb to the pan and fry the rumps on one side for 2–3 minutes until golden, then flip them over and cook for a further 2–3 minutes. Season all over, then pop in the oven for 15 minutes to finish cooking.

Take the pan out of the oven and leave to rest.

Meanwhile, make the mash. Put the riced potatoes, cream and butter in a saucepan and heat gently to warm though. Season and beat together, then set aside.

Make the garlic and seaweed butter. Put the garlic, shallot, butter and seaweed in a medium bowl, season and beat together.

In a saucepan, heat the seaweed butter with 50ml water over a medium heat. When the butter has melted, add all the vegetables and chives to the pan, increase the heat and boil rapidly for 2 minutes. Season well.

To serve, divide the mash between 2 warmed plates and spoon the veg alongside. Slice each lamb rump in half and arrange on the plates, spooning over any resting juices.

Stuffed leg of Welsh lamb with onion and leek sauce

SERVES 8

2kg leg of lamb, boned
sea salt and freshly ground
  black pepper

FOR THE STUFFING
small bunch of flat-leaf parsley,
  chopped
½ small bunch of mint, chopped
4 garlic cloves, finely chopped
150g breadcrumbs
1 tablespoon Dijon mustard
50g hazelnuts, roughly chopped
1 egg
150g black pudding, diced

FOR THE SAUCE
25g salted butter
1 large onion, diced
2 leeks, diced
1 heaped tablespoon plain flour
25ml white wine
400ml full-fat milk
100ml double cream
a few sprigs of flat-leaf parsley,
  chopped

Welsh lamb is without question the best lamb you can get. It is one of the many types of produce that we as a nation need to keep purchasing. Generations and generations of farmers are dotted all around the Welsh hillsides and work tirelessly to get this unbeatable meat to our table. In this dish, I've made a stuffing with parsley, mint and black pudding and rolled it into a leg of lamb. The easiest way to do this at home is to buy a leg of lamb that has been tunnel boned and then you will have a simple pocket to put the stuffing into before you tie it up.

Preheat the oven to 240°C (220°C fan)/475°F/gas 9.

Put the lamb on a board, skin-side down, open out and season all over.

To make the stuffing, put the parsley and mint in the bowl of a food processor and whiz to chop more finely. Add the garlic, breadcrumbs, mustard, hazelnuts and egg and season well. Whiz again to combine.

Spoon the stuffing mixture onto the lamb and spread all over, then scatter over the black pudding and season again. Roll up the lamb to enclose the stuffing, then tie securely with string, both horizontally and vertically. Place on a cooling rack in a large roasting tray and roast for 30 minutes, then reduce the oven to 200°C (180°C fan)/400°F/gas 6 and roast for a further 1 hour. Set aside to rest for 30 minutes.

To make the sauce, heat the butter in a saucepan over a medium heat. Once it is melted and foaming, stir in the diced onion and cook for 5 minutes, stirring regularly. Stir in the leeks and cook for a further 2 minutes. Stir in the flour and cook for 30 seconds–1 minute and season well. Whisk in the wine, milk and cream, season again and stir in the parsley.

Unwrap the lamb and lift onto a board. Slice and serve with the sauce, spooning over any resting juices from the lamb.

PUDDINGS & CAKES

Caramelised rice pudding with strawberries and griddled peaches

SERVES 6

125g salted butter, diced
200g pudding rice
100g caster sugar
450ml full-fat milk
300ml double cream
1 vanilla pod, halved lengthways

FOR THE TOPPING
200g demerara sugar

FOR THE FRUIT
3 peaches, halved and stoned
1 tablespoon vegetable oil
200g strawberries, halved

Beautiful fresh dairy cream is the secret to this sumptuous rice pudding. The rolling pastures of Guernsey certainly provide ample grazing for their cattle herds, which produce the amazingly rich milk that goes into the island's dairy products. I also have to say that cooking this in your own kitchen is a lot easier than in the gale-force winds I had to contend with when we filmed this!

If using, light your BBQ. When the coals are silvery in colour, it's ready to cook on.

Heat a wide, shallow, heavy-based flameproof pan over a medium heat. Add the butter and allow to melt, then pour in the rice and stir well to coat all over. Pour in the sugar, milk and cream, then scrape in the seeds from the vanilla pod and stir everything together. Bring to a simmer and cook for 20 minutes, stirring occasionally.

Once the rice pudding has cooked, sprinkle the demerara sugar all over the top and use a blowtorch to cook the sugar until caramelised. Alternatively, you can do this under a very hot preheated grill.

If not using the BBQ, preheat a griddle pan over a medium heat. Drizzle the cut-side of the peach halves with the vegetable oil and rub all over. Place the peach halves, cut-side down, on the BBQ or griddle pan and cook for 5–6 minutes until golden and slightly charred. Lift into a bowl, add the strawberries and toss together.

Spoon the rice pudding among 6 bowls, then top with the fruit and serve.

Elderflower fritters with poached pears and sabayon

SERVES 4

FOR THE PEARS

4 English pears, peeled, halved
   and cored
1 vanilla pod, halved lengthways
   and seeds scraped
50g caster sugar
100ml elderflower champagne or
   sparkling wine
50ml elderflower cordial
1 lemon, halved
2 tablespoons icing sugar,
   to caramelise

FOR THE SABAYON

5 medium egg yolks
50g caster sugar
25ml elderflower champagne or
   sparkling wine
25ml elderflower cordial

FOR THE FRITTERS

1–2 litres vegetable oil, for frying
50g plain flour
50g cornflour
3 teaspoons caster sugar
200ml elderflower champagne or
   sparkling wine
25ml elderflower cordial
8 heads of elderflower blossom

TO SERVE

2 tablespoons runny honey

These fritters can only be made when elderflowers are in season (look for ones with all the flowers on the head open), but for the rest of the year, the pears and sabayon made with elderflower cordial still make a delicious dessert with a scoop of ice cream. The batter needs to be really thin here for nice, crisp fritters.

Start by poaching the pears. Place the prepared pears in a pan with the vanilla seeds, sugar, elderflower champagne or sparkling wine and cordial. Pour in 300ml water, then squeeze the juice from the lemon halves into the pan and drop the squeezed pieces in, too. Bring to the boil over a medium heat, then simmer for 10 minutes. Drain and set the pears aside to cool.

Place the cooled pears on a baking tray, dust with the icing sugar then use a blowtorch to caramelise the sugar. Alternatively, you can do this under a very hot preheated grill.

Next, make the sabayon. Put the egg yolks into a large heatproof bowl and add the sugar, elderflower champagne and cordial. Rest the bowl over a pan of just-simmering water, set over a low-medium heat, making sure the base doesn't touch the water. Whisk continuously for around 5 minutes using either a balloon whisk or electric hand whisk, until the mixture has thickened and is light and moussey.

Heat the vegetable oil in a deep-fat fryer to 170°C/340°F or in a deep heavy-based saucepan until a breadcrumb sizzles and turns brown when dropped into it. (Note: hot oil can be dangerous; do not leave unattended). Line a large plate with kitchen paper.

To make the fritters, combine the flour, cornflour and 1 teaspoon of the caster sugar in a bowl, stir in the elderflower champagne or sparkling wine and cordial and mix until smooth. Try not to overwhisk the mixture, or the batter will be tough.

Dip a couple of elderflower heads into the batter and carefully lower into the hot oil. Fry for 1 minute until golden and crisp. Lift out with a slotted spoon to drain on the kitchen paper. Sprinkle each with a little of the remaining caster sugar. Repeat until you've fried all the elderflowers.

To serve, place the pears onto a large oval platter and spoon over the sabayon. Use the blowtorch to briefly colour the sabayon and pears, then drizzle with the honey and top with the fritters.

Strawberry and raspberry Charlotte Royale

SERVES 8

1 teaspoon olive oil or vegetable oil

3 x 20-cm ready-made Swiss roll cakes, each cut into 5-mm slices

200g raspberries

FOR THE MOUSSE

16 gelatine leaves

500ml good-quality fresh custard

300ml good-quality strawberry or raspberry sauce

6 egg whites

600ml double cream

TO SERVE

200g mixed summer fruit (strawberries, raspberries and redcurrants)

a few sprigs of fresh mint

Charlotte Royale is one of two classic desserts that are made in a similar way: Charlotte Russe uses the same mousse filling, but is lined with sponge fingers, rather than Swiss roll. Either would make a great dessert to eat sat by the riverbank in Oxford, I thought… well, until a coachload of screaming kids turned up, which ruined the illusion. It aged Ryan the soundman by several years, trying to compete with the ever-growing crescendo of noise! Perhaps you will find a more peaceful setting to enjoy this summer favourite.

Put the gelatine for the mousse into a bowl of cold water and leave to soak for 5 minutes.

Meanwhile, brush the oil all over the inside of a 3-litre glass bowl, then line with clingfilm, smoothing it out and pressing right to the edges. Arrange the slices of Swiss roll inside the bowl, so they cover the sides completely. Set aside.

Back to the mousse. In a medium saucepan, gently warm the custard over a low heat. Lift the gelatine out of the bowl and squeeze out any excess water, then add to the pan of warmed custard. Add the strawberry or raspberry sauce and continue to gently heat, stirring until the gelatine has completely dissolved. Remove the pan from the heat and set aside to cool.

Meanwhile, whisk the egg whites in a spotlessly clean bowl to stiff peaks. Whip the double cream in a separate bowl.

When the custard mixture is cool, fold in the cream with a large metal spoon, then fold in the egg whites, mixing carefully until you have a smooth mousse.

Fill the bottom of the sponge-lined bowl with the raspberries, then spoon over the mousse and level the top. Cover with clingfilm and chill for at least 4 hours and up to 24 hours.

When ready to serve, upturn the bowl onto a large platter or cake stand. Lift off the bowl and remove the clingfilm, then decorate with the strawberries, raspberries, redcurrants and mint sprigs.

COUNTY ARMAGH, NORTHERN IRELAND

Lindisfarne mead parfait with hazelnut praline and blackberries

SERVES 8

FOR THE PARFAIT
2 gelatine leaves
500ml double cream
6 egg yolks
200g caster sugar
75ml Lindisfarne mead

FOR THE PRALINE
100g caster sugar
100g hazelnuts

FOR THE MEAD GEL
100ml Lindisfarne mead
1 tablespoon xanthan gum

FOR THE BLACKBERRY GEL
100g blackberries
1 tablespoon xanthan gum

TO SERVE
1 x 500-ml tub blackberry sorbet
8 blackberries, halved
a few purple shiso leaves
  or mint sprigs

Mead is still made in the surrounding areas of the Holy Island of Lindisfarne on the east coast of England. This delicious alcoholic beverage made by fermenting honey has fallen out of favour over the years. I don't know why, as it is truly wonderful, especially in this stunning dessert. You can buy it online – try it.

Start by making the parfait. Put the gelatine into a bowl of cold water and soak for 5 minutes. Meanwhile, pour the cream into a large bowl and whisk until soft peaks form. This is easiest to do with an electric hand whisk but take care not to overwhip the cream.

Put the egg yolks and caster sugar into a large bowl and rest over a saucepan of simmering water, making sure the base isn't touching the water. Whisk the yolks and sugar until the mixture has thickened and doubled in size and leaves a ribbon-like trail when the whisk is lifted.

Lift the gelatine out of the water and squeeze out any excess liquid. Whisk into the egg yolk mixture, then remove the bowl from the pan to cool slightly. Fold in the whipped cream and Lindisfarne mead.

Line a large tray with a non-stick mat and place 8 x 10-cm ring moulds on top, then divide the parfait mixture among the moulds. Freeze for at least 2 hours, ideally overnight.

Meanwhile, make the gels. Place the mead and xanthan gum into a blender and blitz for 2–3 minutes until smooth. The blackberry gel is made in the same way, but blitz the blackberries a little first before adding the xanthan gum. Spoon each gel into a separate piping bag.

Next, make the praline. Line a deep baking tray with another non-stick mat. Heat the sugar and hazelnuts together in a heavy-based pan over a medium heat until the sugar has melted and turned a golden caramel colour. Pour the caramel and nuts onto the non-stick mat and set aside to cool. When cool, blitz the praline in a food processor to a fine crumb, then tip onto a plate.

To serve, dip each of the parfaits, still in their rings, into the praline crumb. Warm the rings in your hands to release the parfaits, then pop each into the centre of a dessert plate. Pipe alternate gel dots around the outside of each parfait, then decorate each with a spoonful of sorbet, 2 blackberry halves and a few purple shiso leaves or mint sprigs.

210

Tuile baskets with ice cream and bubbly chocolate shards

SERVES 6

FOR THE TUILE BASKETS
115g salted butter, softened
140g icing sugar
3 egg whites
115g plain flour

TO SERVE
1 x 500-ml tub vanilla ice cream
1 x 200-g tub clotted cream
around 300g mixed berries
a few mint sprigs
store-bought strawberry sauce
2 x bars of store-bought bubbly
   mint chocolate (such as Aero)
   or see the tip and ingredients
   below for the homemade version

**FOR THE HOMEMADE BUBBLY
MINT CHOCOLATE (OPTIONAL)**
500g dark chocolate,
   broken up into pieces
200g food-safe cocoa butter/
   cacao butter
a few drops of mint extract

I got the idea for this from Jelberts of Newlyn. Well, it's ice cream and clotted cream… what's not to like?

Put the butter into a large bowl, add the icing sugar and beat together until smooth. Gradually beat in the egg whites, then fold in the flour. Transfer to the fridge to chill for 30 minutes.

Preheat the oven to 200°C (180°C fan)/400°F/gas 6 and line a large baking sheet with baking parchment.

Divide the tuile mixture into 6 portions and spoon onto the lined baking sheet, spacing them well apart. Use the back of the spoon or a palette knife to smooth into 6 thin circles, about 15cm in diameter. Bake for 5 minutes until the tuiles look firm and very slightly golden around the edges.

Working quickly, carefully lift each tuile off the baking sheet with a palette knife and place each over a small upturned bowl to form basket shapes. Leave to cool and set.

To serve, place each basket on a serving plate and fill each with a scoop of ice cream, a dollop of clotted cream, a handful of berries and a few mint sprigs. Drizzle over the strawberry sauce and sprinkle a few pieces of the bubbly chocolate on top and around the outside.

JAMES'S TIP
To make your own bubbly mint chocolate requires some specialist kit, including a vacuum-packing machine. Put the chocolate, cocoa/cacao butter and mint extract into a bowl resting over a pan of simmering water (ensure the base of the bowl does not touch the water) for 15 minutes until everything is melted. If you have a sugar thermometer, try to keep the temperature at 50°C. Pour the mixture into a warmed whipped cream siphon or espuma gun. Charge with 2 x No.2 charges, then dispense the mixture into a vacuum-sealable container, filling it no more than halfway. Seal, then place the container under vacuum according to the manufacturer's instructions until the desired bubbly texture is achieved. Freeze for 1 hour, then it's ready to use.

DAIRY ICE-CREAM
HOME-MADE
FRESH DAILY
CONES- £1·20
+
£1·60

TUBS £1·70
+
£2·70

Forest gin and fruit jellies

SERVES 8–10

FOR THE JELLY
10 gelatine leaves
100ml Forest gin
120ml elderflower cordial
50g caster sugar
400g raspberries
400g mixed berries, such as
  strawberries, blackberries,
  redcurrants and blueberries

TO SERVE
1 x 500-ml tub raspberry sorbet
a few mint sprigs

I visited two great gin distilleries on my travels for this series. To honest, I could have done a whole series on gin. Toad Gin in Oxford and Forest Gin in the Peak District provided some highlights as well as headaches! I love this dessert, as it is basically a grown-up version of jelly and ice cream.

Put the gelatine leaves into a large bowl, pour over enough cold water to cover and leave to soak for 2–3 minutes.

Pour the gin into a large pan, along with the elderflower cordial and sugar. Pour in 400ml water and heat gently over a low-medium heat to dissolve the sugar. Lift the gelatine leaves out of the bowl and squeeze out any excess water, then add to the pan and whisk in. Pour half the liquid into a separate bowl and set aside to make the elderflower and gin jellies (this step is optional – if you'd like all the jellies to be raspberry-flavoured, you can omit this).

Add most of the raspberries to the remaining liquid in the pan, saving a few for decoration. Press down on the raspberries with the back of a metal spoon to extract the juices.

Line a sieve with muslin and rest over a bowl. Pour the warm raspberry liquid mixture into the sieve and strain through the muslin.

Divide the mixed berries, including the reserved raspberries, between 8–10 small jelly moulds (these can be any shape you like – have fun!). Pour the jelly mixture/s between the moulds, then chill in the fridge for 1 hour until set.

When ready to serve, briefly dip the moulds into hot water and turn out each jelly onto a dessert plate. Serve with sorbet and decorated with mint sprigs.

Barry Island churros with two dipping sauces

SERVES 6

FOR THE CHOCOLATE ORANGE SAUCE
100g dark chocolate, chopped
zest and juice of 1 orange
100ml double cream

FOR THE WHISKY CARAMEL SAUCE
1 x 397-g jar dulce de leche
50ml whisky cream liqueur

FOR THE CHURROS
1–2 litres vegetable oil, for frying
75g salted butter
250g plain flour
1 egg
1 teaspoon baking powder

TO SERVE
cocoa powder and caster sugar,
  for sprinkling

In recent years, Barry Island has become famous as the setting for the TV comedy series 'Gavin and Stacey', but it has been a favourite holiday destination for Brits for centuries. I love classic British seaside resorts, so I couldn't resist having a go on the funfair that sits at the heart of the island. These churros make for perfect funfair snacking.

For the chocolate orange sauce, put the chocolate, orange zest and juice and cream into a small heavy-based saucepan and heat gently over a very low heat until the chocolate has melted. Gently stir together, then pour the sauce into a bowl.

For the whisky caramel sauce, combine the dulce de leche and cream liqueur in a pan and heat gently over a low heat, stirring every now and then, until gently bubbling. Pour into a separate bowl.

To make the churros, heat the vegetable oil in a deep-fat fryer to 180°C/350°F or in a deep heavy-based saucepan until a breadcrumb sizzles and turns brown when dropped into it. (Note: hot oil can be dangerous; do not leave unattended.) Line a large plate with kitchen paper.

Put the butter into a medium saucepan, pour in 325ml water and place over a low heat. Once the butter has melted and the water comes to a rolling boil, beat in the flour. Cook over the heat for about 1 minute, then remove the pan from the heat. Beat in the egg and finally the baking powder. Spoon the mixture into a piping bag fitted with a 1-cm star nozzle.

Carefully pipe lengths of the churro mixture into the hot oil, using a pair of scissors to snip each one off from the nozzle at about 10cm long. Cook in batches of 3 or 4 at a time, frying for 1–2 minutes until golden brown, then lift out with a slotted spoon to drain on the kitchen paper. Dust the hot churros with cocoa and sprinkle with caster sugar as you go. Repeat until all the mixture has been used up.

Serve the still-hot churros with the sauces for dipping.

Lammas fairground donuts with whiskey syrup and caramel popcorn

MAKES 12

FOR THE WHISKEY SYRUP
300g caster sugar
50ml Irish whiskey

FOR THE DONUTS
300ml milk
500g strong plain bread flour,
   plus extra for dusting
75g caster sugar
1 teaspoon sea salt
1 sachet (7g) dried active yeast
   (or 14g fresh yeast, crumbled)
1 egg, beaten
50g salted butter, softened
1–2 litres vegetable oil, for frying
6 fudge squares
6 raspberries
squirty cream, to decorate

FOR THE POPCORN
1 tablespoon vegetable oil
50g popcorn kernels
50g dulce de leche

Another fairground classic, I cooked this dish at the annual Auld Lammas Fair in Ballycastle. Ireland's oldest fair, it features traditional music, horse trading, plenty of artisan food stalls and the all-important funfair. It attracts well over 100,000 visitors every year. To be honest, it did feel like more than that, as we tried to find the quietest part of town to cook in – right at the end of the pier in the shadow of the ferris wheel.

First, make the syrup. Put the sugar into a medium saucepan and pour in 200ml water. Heat gently to dissolve the sugar, then bring to the boil. Stir in the whiskey, take the pan off the heat and set aside to cool.

Next, make the donuts. Put the milk, flour, sugar, salt, yeast, egg and butter into a large bowl. Stir everything together, then use your hands to knead to a rough dough. Turn out onto a clean work surface and knead until smooth, then transfer to a clean bowl, cover in clingfilm or a clean tea towel and leave to prove in a warm place for 2 hours.

Heat the vegetable oil in a deep-fat fryer to 170°C/340°F or in a deep heavy-based saucepan until a breadcrumb sizzles and turns brown when dropped into it. (Note: hot oil can be dangerous; do not leave unattended.) Line a large plate with kitchen paper.

Turn the donut dough out onto a lightly floured work surface and divide into 12 even-sized pieces. Using a little extra flour, take each one and shape into a disc, flatten slightly and place a piece of fudge or a raspberry into the middle. Enclose the dough around the filling and roll into a ball. Continue until you've filled and shaped all the dough.

Working in batches, carefully lower the donuts into the hot oil and fry for 3–4 minutes, turning occasionally. Lift out with a slotted spoon to drain on the kitchen paper, then pop into the whiskey syrup and leave to soak for a minute before transferring to a serving platter.

Meanwhile, make the popcorn. Heat a large non-stick saucepan with a lid and add the oil and popcorn. Cover with the lid and cook until all the corn has popped, shaking the pan occasionally. Once the corn has stopped popping, remove the lid and stir through the dulce de leche.

To serve, spoon more syrup over the donuts and decorate with squirty cream and a sprinkling of popcorn.

Apple pie with honey cream

SERVES 6–8

FOR THE PASTRY
450g plain flour,
  plus extra for rolling out
¼ teaspoon salt
4 tablespoons icing sugar
200g cold salted butter, cubed
2 eggs, beaten
2 tablespoons iced water

FOR THE EGG WASH
1 egg, beaten

FOR THE FILLING
6 English eating apples, peeled,
  cored and diced
2 Bramley apples, peeled, cored
  and diced
100g golden caster sugar,
  plus 1–2 tablespoons for sprinkling
2 tablespoons local runny honey

TO SERVE
500ml double cream
2 tablespoons local runny honey

There has been a lot written about the importance of bees in recent years and I am not going to repeat it here, but just say that without them the world wouldn't be the same and apples are one of the many things that require bees to do their thing. You can support British honey producers by using local honey in the filling for this delicious apple pie which is also served with a lovely honey cream. The key to making the best apple pie is to make sure that your pastry ingredients are as cold as possible. In America, where I learned how to make the best apple pie from the person who sends one to each new president when they get elected, they often freeze the flour as well as the butter to keep it cold.

Preheat the oven to 190°C (170°C fan)/375°F/gas 5.

To make the pastry, mix the flour, salt and icing sugar together in a large bowl. Add the butter and use your fingertips to rub the butter in lightly until the mixture resembles breadcrumbs. Add the beaten eggs and water and stir in with your hands to combine, then very lightly knead the mixture to bring together to make a dough. Form the pastry into a ball, then wrap in clingfilm and pop in the fridge for 30 minutes.

Lightly flour a clean work surface. Roll out one third of the dough until it is large enough to line a 23-cm deep fluted pie dish. Fill with the prepared apples, sprinkle the 100g of golden caster sugar over the top and dot with the honey.

Roll out the remaining two-thirds of the pastry so that it's just large enough to cover the pie dish. Use a pastry brush to brush the edge of the pastry in the dish with a little egg wash, then carefully lay the circle of pastry over the top. Trim off any excess pastry, then crimp the edges. Shape any leftover pastry into leaves and use to decorate the pie. Brush the egg wash all over to cover, then sprinkle over the remaining 1–2 tablespoons of caster sugar.

Transfer to the bottom shelf of the oven and bake for 1 hour.

To serve, whisk the cream and honey together in a large bowl until softly whipped (alternatively, whip the cream and then just drizzle over the honey). Serve the pie with the honey cream on the side.

Singing hinnies with lemon cream

MAKES 12

450g plain flour,
    plus extra for rolling out
1 teaspoon baking powder
½ teaspoon cream of tartar
½ teaspoon salt
110g salted butter, diced,
    plus a little extra for frying
110g lard, diced, plus a little
    extra for frying
zest of 1 lemon
185g mixed dried fruits
120ml milk
a little caster sugar, for sprinkling

FOR THE LEMON CREAM
150g full-fat cream cheese
100ml crème fraîche
200g lemon curd

You are probably wondering what Singing Hinnies are. Well, they are a kind of griddle cake from Northumberland and the name comes from the noise that they make while they are cooking – sizzling and 'singing' – and 'hinny' is how they say 'honey' in these parts – a sweet term of endearment. The reason they are in this book is because of Sam Head. Sam has worked with me for over 20 years and is a local lass, but don't ask her for directions, because really, she hasn't got a clue where anything is… even in her hometown!

Tip the flour into a large bowl. Add the baking powder, cream of tartar and salt, and stir everything together. Stir in the butter and lard, then rub the fats into the flour with your fingertips until the mixture looks like breadcrumbs. Add the lemon zest and dried fruits, then sprinkle over the milk and use your hands to bring all the ingredients together into a soft dough.

Lightly dust a board and rolling pin with flour, then roll out the dough until it measures around 3mm thick. Stamp out circles using an 8-cm cutter, re-rolling the dough as you go.

Heat a flat griddle pan or a heavy-based frying pan over a high heat until hot, then add a little butter and lard. Once melted and the butter is foaming, reduce the heat to medium, pop the rounds in the pan and cook in batches for 2–3 minutes on each side.

Place the hot singing hinnies on a serving plate and sprinkle with a little caster sugar.

To make the cream, mix the cream cheese and crème fraîche together in a bowl until well combined, then swirl through the lemon curd. Serve alongside the singing hinnies.

Apple fritters with cider custard and cider butter

SERVES 6

FOR THE CUSTARD
600ml double cream
100ml cider
1 vanilla pod, halved lengthways
75g caster sugar
8 egg yolks

FOR THE FRITTERS
1–2 litres vegetable oil, for frying
250g plain flour
50g cornflour
pinch of ground cinnamon
1 tablespoon runny honey
350ml cider (sweet or
    dry – your choice)
3 red English apples, cored
    and sliced into 1-cm thick rings
caster sugar, for sprinkling

FOR THE CIDER BUTTER
100g softened salted butter
100g icing sugar, sifted
25ml cider (sweet or
    dry – your choice)

TO SERVE
edible flowers

These are made with the brilliant Welsh Mountain Cider I found on my trip, which I now use in my restaurant, and is from one of the highest apple orchards in the country, in Llanidloes, Wales. It's not the cheapest of ciders, but – my god – compared to the stuff of student hangovers, it's miles apart. If you can find it, buy it.

Start by making the custard. Pour the cream and cider into a medium heavy-based pan. Scrape the seeds from the vanilla pod into the pan and stir in, then add half of the sugar. Set over a low heat and cook just until it almost comes to the boil (there will be a few bubbles around the edge), then immediately remove the pan from the heat.

Meanwhile, whisk the egg yolks in a large bowl with the remaining sugar until just smooth. Pour in the cream mixture, whisking continuously until well combined, then pour the mixture back into the pan. Set back over a low heat and warm through, continuing to whisk. When the bubbles are disappearing on top, it's ready. Strain the mixture through a sieve into a bowl, then set aside.

To make the cider butter, beat all the ingredients together in a bowl until smooth, then set aside.

Heat the vegetable oil for the fritters in a deep-fat fryer to 170°C/340°F or in a deep heavy-based saucepan until a breadcrumb sizzles and turns brown when dropped into it. (Note: hot oil can be dangerous; do not leave unattended.) Line a large plate with kitchen paper.

To make the batter, sift the flour, cornflour and cinnamon into a medium bowl, then add the honey and pour in the cider. Quickly whisk together until smooth, taking care not to overbeat or the batter will have a tough texture. Use a fork to dip the apple rings into the batter, then carefully transfer to the hot oil and fry, in batches, for 2–3 minutes until golden and crispy. Lift out with a slotted spoon to drain on the kitchen paper, then sprinkle with caster sugar.

To serve, divide the custard among 6 plates and top with the fritters, followed by a spoonful of butter and a sprinkling of edible flowers to decorate.

Millionaire's shortbread

MAKES 12

FOR THE BISCUIT BASE
300g salted butter, softened
200g dark soft brown sugar
350g plain flour
125g cornflour

FOR THE CARAMEL FILLING
1 x 397-g jar dulce de leche
250g salted butter
150g caster sugar

FOR THE TOPPING
400g dark chocolate (70% cocoa solids), broken into pieces
100g salted butter

For this recipe I have to thank Kj, the Head Chef and owner of the Mountain Café in Aviemore. Kirsten Gilmore is a long way from her native New Zealand but now has a reputation for food, service and kick-ass coffee (in her own words!) with an amazing view of the Cairngorm Mountains in Scotland. You have to order the fish chowder and the sweetcorn fritters and, without a doubt, the best millionaire's shortbread I have ever tasted. She kindly gave me her recipe, so here it is for you.

Preheat the oven to 170°C (150°C fan)/325°F/gas 3.

To make the biscuit base, put the butter, sugar and both types of flour into a large bowl. Use your fingertips to rub the butter into the other ingredients until the mixture looks really crumbly. Press the mixture into a 23 x 30-cm loose-bottomed cake tin (no need to line) and use a palette knife to even out the surface. Bake for 20 minutes, then remove from the oven and cool in the tin on a wire rack.

To make the caramel filling, combine the dulce de leche, butter and sugar in a large saucepan over a medium heat. Whisking the mixture, bring to the boil (be careful as the mixture will be extremely hot). Pour evenly over the biscuit base, cover and leave to set for at least 4 hours or overnight at room temperature.

To make the topping, put the chocolate and butter into a medium heavy-based pan and gently heat. Once everything has melted, whisk to combine. Cool slightly, then pour over the caramel and level with a palette knife. Cover, then leave to set overnight at room temperature.

Cut into 12 squares to serve.

Black butter and apple Bakewell tart

SERVES 6–8

FOR THE PASTRY

225g plain flour,
  plus extra for dusting
pinch of salt
2 tablespoons icing sugar
100g cold salted butter, cubed,
  plus extra for greasing
1 egg, beaten
1 tablespoon iced water

FOR THE FILLING

4 tablespoons black butter preserve
225g softened salted butter
225g caster sugar
4 eggs, beaten
175g ground almonds
50g plain flour
2 English apples, cored and
  thinly sliced

FOR THE GLAZE

1½ tablespoons caster sugar
1½ tablespoons boiling water

TO SERVE

Jersey cream, whipped

In the Channel Islands, I went to see how Jersey black butter was made. It's not actually made with butter – to be honest there's none in it at all. In fact, it's a preserve made with top-quality apples, liquorice, spices and sugar, which is cooked in the traditional way over a firepit and stirred all the time to prevent it from burning. As it slowly cooks it develops an amazing, caramelised, sweet flavour. It is not only great in this tart, but also fabulous served on its own, spread on toast or scones.

To make the pastry, sift the flour and salt into a bowl. Stir in the icing sugar, then add the butter. Use your fingertips to rub the butter into the flour mixture until it resembles breadcrumbs. Mix in the egg and water using a round-bladed table knife, then gently bring the mixture together into a ball. Wrap in clingfilm and pop in the fridge for 30 minutes.

Preheat the oven to 180°C (160°C fan)/350°F/gas 4. Grease a 23-cm fluted tart tin lightly with butter.

Dust a little flour over a clean work surface and roll out the pastry into a large round big enough to line the tart tin. Lift into the tin and press into the edges gently. Trim away the excess pastry, then spoon the black butter preserve for the filling into the base. Use the back of the spoon to spread it out to cover the pastry dough.

Make the filling by beating the butter and sugar together in a large bowl. Mix in the eggs, then fold in the ground almonds and flour. Spoon the mixture evenly over the black butter and layer the apple slices over the top.

Bake for 35–40 minutes until golden, then remove from the oven and leave to cool to room temperature in the tin.

Meanwhile, make the glaze. Pop the sugar and boiling water into a small pan and heat, stirring until the sugar has dissolved.

Brush the tart with the glaze, then carefully remove from the tin to a serving plate. Slice and serve with the cream.

Duck-egg sponge with blackberry jam

SERVES 8

FOR THE CAKE
250g salted butter, softened,
  plus extra for greasing
250g caster sugar
4 duck eggs, beaten
250g self-raising flour

FOR THE JAM
300g blackberries
300g caster sugar

TO DECORATE
handful of blackberries/brambles
  (with leaves if you like),
  to decorate
icing sugar, to dust

Salakee Farm is based in St Mary's on the Isles of Scilly and is a small farm where three generations have raised Salakee ducks, which are sold for meat but also produce amazing duck eggs. I spent most of the day on my visit here trying to find the eggs in amongst the hedgerows, so this cake very much has a hedgerow theme to it.

Grease and line 2 x 23-cm cake tins with greaseproof paper. Preheat the oven to 180°C (160°C fan)/350°F/gas 4.

Beat the softened butter and sugar together in a large bowl, using either a wooden spoon or an electric hand whisk, until the mixture looks pale and creamy. Gradually add the eggs, a little at a time, beating well after each addition. Sift over the flour and gently fold in until the mixture looks smooth.

Divide the cake batter evenly between the lined tins and roughly level off with the back of the spoon. If you gently drop each tin onto the work surface it will help level off the mixture completely. Bake for 25–30 minutes or until a skewer or cocktail stick inserted into the centre comes out clean. Cool in the tins for 5 minutes, then turn each cake out onto a wire rack to cool completely, removing the greaseproof paper.

Meanwhile, make the jam. Put the blackberries and sugar into a large saucepan and heat gently to dissolve the sugar. Bring to the boil, then simmer for 15 minutes until you have a jam, then set aside to cool.

Place one of the sponges onto a large serving plate or cake plate and spoon the jam on top, spreading it out to the edges. Sit the other sponge on top and decorate with blackberries, a few leaves (if using – watch out for thorns!) and a dusting of icing sugar.

Banana and ice-cream cake

SERVES 8

FOR THE BANANA CAKE
200g salted butter,
  at room temperature,
  plus extra for greasing
200g caster sugar
2 ripe bananas
3 eggs
200g self-raising flour

FOR THE FILLING
2 litres vanilla ice cream,
  softened slightly
300ml double cream

FOR THE TOPPING
500g dark chocolate (70% cocoa
  solids), broken into pieces
1 tablespoon salted butter
1 x 200-g tub clotted cream

This idea came from eating Jelberts ice cream in Newlyn, Penzance. Owner Jimmy Glover sells vanilla ice cream and that's it. Well, with the option of a flake and a massive dollop of clotted cream, and wow – it's good. This is like a massive choc-ice and can be served for one, as 'James the mad dog' on our crew proved.

Preheat the oven to 180°C (160°C fan)/350°F/gas 4. Grease and line a 23-cm round deep springform cake tin with greaseproof paper.

First make the cake. Put the butter and sugar into the bowl of a freestanding mixer and beat together until the mixture turns creamy and white. You can also do this in a large bowl with an electric hand whisk. Add the bananas and beat the mixture until smooth, then beat in the eggs. Sift the flour into the bowl, then fold into the mixture using a large metal spoon.

Spoon the cake batter into the prepared tin, level the surface and bake for 40 minutes. Let the cake cool in the tin for 5 minutes, then turn out onto a wire rack to cool completely.

Leaving the lining paper on the cooled cake, transfer it to a board and slice horizontally into 3 rounds. Place the lined bottom layer of the cake back onto the base of the tin and spoon half of the ice cream on top, smoothing it over and levelling it out. Place the middle layer of cake on top of this, then spoon the rest of the ice cream on top, smoothing it over as before. Place the last layer of cake on top.

Whip the double cream in a medium bowl until stiff peaks form. Spread it all over the sides and top of the cake and level off, then transfer the cake to the freezer for 4 hours until set firm.

When ready to serve, melt the chocolate and butter for the topping in a heatproof bowl resting over a pan of just-simmering water, making sure the base doesn't touch the water. Place the cake on a cake rack set over a baking tray, then pour the melted chocolate mixture all over the cake to cover, letting any excess chocolate drip into the tray below. The topping will set on contact with the frozen cake. Once set, spoon the clotted cream on top to decorate. Transfer the cake to a serving plate, and let sit for about 15 minutes before serving in slices.

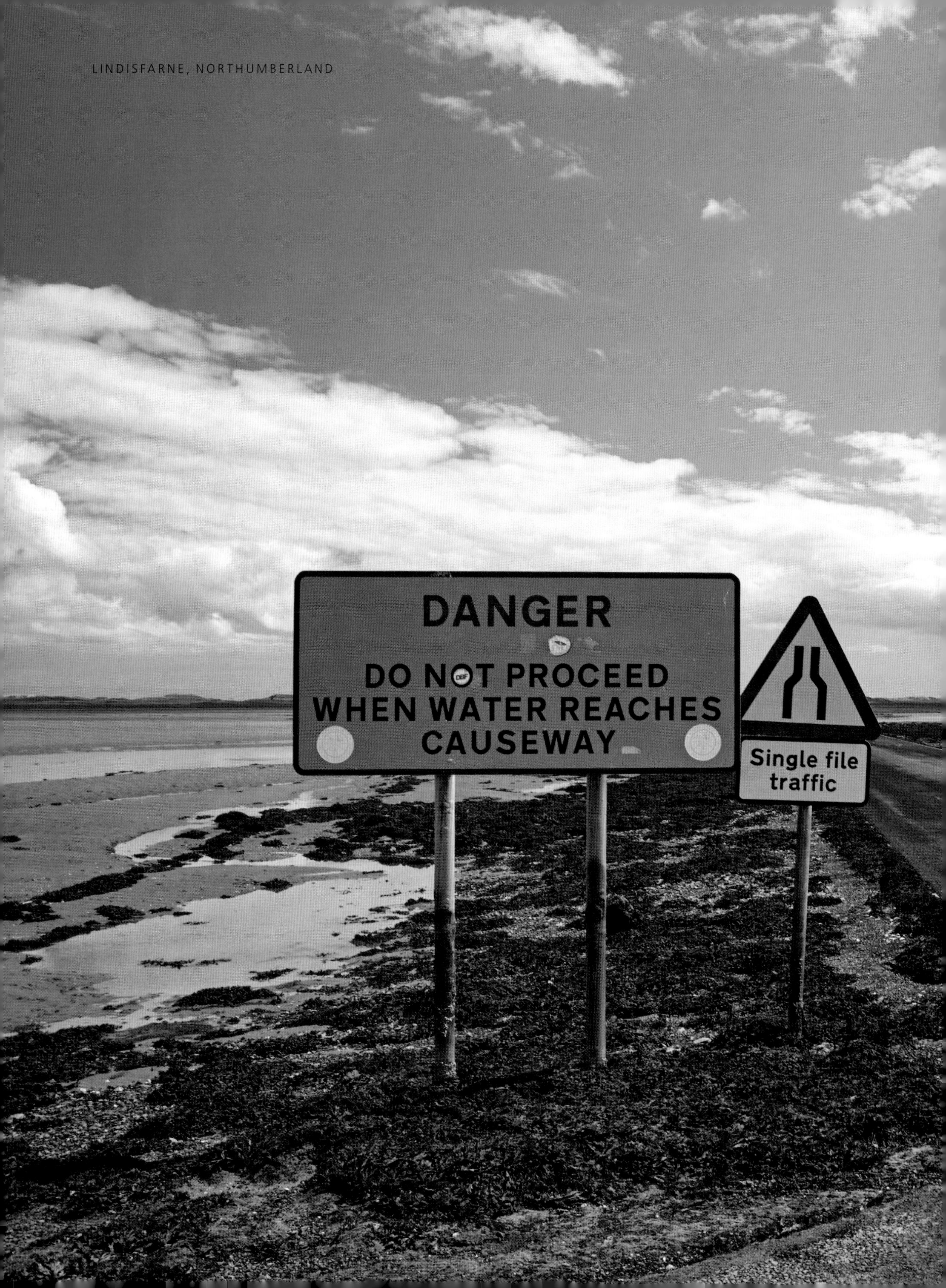

LINDISFARNE, NORTHUMBERLAND

With thanks to all the producers and suppliers featured on the show

ISLES OF SCILLY

SC Salt
Sea salt made from the crystal-clear waters of St Martin's Par Beach.
sc-salt.co.uk

Tanglewood Table at the Post Office
A post office in St Mary's with a tiny 8-cover restaurant at the back!
tanglewoodkitchen.co.uk

Salakee Farm
Owners Kylie and Dave raise Salakee ducks in small batches on their farm in St Mary's.
salakeefarm.co.uk

CORNWALL

Jelberts
One of the oldest ice cream makers in the country, situated in Newlyn, Penzance and owned by Jim Glover and family.

Fresh Cornish Fish
Family fishmonger in Newlyn, Penzance, for well over 30 years, sourcing and supplying Cornish fish fresh from Newlyn market every day.
fresh-cornish-fish.co.uk

DEVON

Forest Fungi
Farm shop and café in Dawlish, where they grow mushrooms in their 'Shroom Rooms' on site.
forestfungi.co.uk

Sharpham Wine & Cheese
An estate near Totnes, with Jersey cows and a vineyard, producing award-winning cheese and wine.
sharpham.com

JERSEY

Jersey Royal Potatoes
The Jersey Royal potato enjoys EU protection of designation in origin thanks to Jersey's unique growing conditions.
jerseyroyals.co.uk

Jersey Oyster
The world's first ASC-certified oyster farm offering responsible and sustainably farmed oysters all year round. Also supplier of mussels.
jerseyoyster.com

La Mare Wine Estate
Established in 1972, an estate with vineyards and orchards producing their own wine and cider, chocolate, black butter and preserves.
lamarewineestate.com

GUERNSEY

Senners Bakery
Bakery selling the traditional Guernsey gâche and other breads and cakes.

Golden Guernsey Goat's Cheese
Mandy and Peter Girard make cheese from the milk of the rare Golden Guernsey goats on their farm.

Le Petit Bistro
Authentic French restaurant in the heart of St Peter Port.
petitbistro.co.uk

DORSET

Dorset Blue Vinny
The Davies family have been making award-winning Dorset Blue Vinny at Woodbridge Farm, Sturminster Newton, for almost 40 years.
dorsetblue.com

The Salt Pig
An urban farm shop and café in Wareham, owned by James Warren who also breeds Mangalitza pigs in Arne.
thesaltpig.co.uk

OXFORD

Medley Manor Farm
One of only three farms left in Oxford. Acquired by Charlie Gee's father in 1958, they grow fruit and veg, offer PYO raspberries and strawberries, and have bee hives.
medleymanorfarm.co.uk

Toad
The Oxford Artisan Distillery uses ancient heritage grain, all sustainably grown on organic farms within a 50-mile radius of their site, to make unique gin and vodka.
spiritoftoad.com

2 North Parade
Victoria Borondo and Peter Slade's neighbourhood produce store in Oxford, stocking produce from local farmers, producers and suppliers.
2northparade.com

WALES

Beacons Farm Shop at the Welsh Venison Centre
Andrew and Elaine Morgan sell their award-winning lamb, venison, beef and pork in their farm shop in the Brecon Beacons National Park, as well as supplying restaurants and hotels nationwide.
beaconsfarmshop.co.uk

Welsh Mountain Cider & Tree Nursery
Bill Bleasdale and Chava Richman grow fruit trees in Llanidloes and make sulphite-free cider that has been fermented in barrels over 6 to 18 months.
welshmountaincider.com

Ifor's Welsh Wagyu Farm
Ifor Humphreys raises award-winning Wagyu beef cattle on the clover-rich pastures of Montgomery to produce meat with a unique taste and texture and a superior marbling of fat.
iforswelshwagyu.co.uk

PEAK DISTRICT

Forest Distillery
A 17th century barn and distillery high up in the Macclesfield Forest where they make gin and whisky.
theforestdistillery.com

YORKSHIRE DALES

The Grid Iron Meat Co
Sources native-breed meat from North Yorkshire farms and offers meat and homemade charcuterie, such as Yorkshire frankfurters, made from selective native breeds.
gridironmeat.co.uk

LAKE DISTRICT

Sharrow Bay
Restaurant by Ullswater where sticky toffee pudding was first created by Francis Coulson in the 1970s.
sharrowbay.co.uk

Lake District Farmers
Supply premium, breed-specific meat from 50 Lake District farmers to select world-class and Michelin Star restaurants in the UK.
lakedistrictfarmers.co.uk

NORTHUMBERLAND

Swallowfish
Shop and smokehouse that has been operating in Seahouses since 1843. They still use the same methods of smoking today, with oak sawdust and no additives, preservatives or colourings.
swallowfish.co.uk

Lindisfarne Mead
St Aidan's Winery is the home of Lindisfarne mead, a unique fortified wine made from fermented white grapes, honey, herbs and fine spirits.
lindisfarne.org.uk/mead

Northumberland Seafood Centre
Sources seafood directly from local fishermen, taking the strain off overfished stocks and introducing customers to new types of seafood that may be more sustainable.
northumberlandseafood.co.uk

ISLE OF MAN

Apple Orphanage
In 2009, Will Faulds and Charlotte Traynor started taking donations from apple-tree owners across the island and giving juice in return.
appleorphanage.com

Close Leece Farm
Family farm that breeds Tamworth pigs, Golden Guernsey goats, chickens and Loaghton lamb, which is indigenous to the Isle of Man. They make pork chorizo, lamb salami and air-dried charcuterie.
closeleecefarm.com

NORTHERN IRELAND

Broughgammon Farm
A forward-thinking farm in Co. Antrim that takes the male kid goats born to the dairy industry and rears them for cabrito kid goat meat. They now also rear free-range rose veal and seasonal wild game.
broughgammon.com

Islander Rathlin Kelp
Here they grow three varieties of kelp native to Rathlin Island: sugar kelp, kombu and wakame. They also sell their own kelp-based products.
islanderkelp.com

Wasabi Crop
Father and son team, Sean and Zak, grow wasabi in their back garden and they are the only commercial grower of wasabi in Ireland.
wasabicrop.com

Yellow Door
A catering company in County Armagh for 25 years, Yellow Door's kitchen garden boasts edible flowers, salad leaves, micro herbs, a small orchard, fruit bushes and four colonies of bees, from which they get their wonderful honey.
yellowdoordeli.co.uk

Lough Neagh Fishermen's Co-operative
One of the forerunners of wild eel producers and recognised as the largest producer of wild-caught eel in Europe. Lough Neagh is the largest freshwater lake in the UK and Ireland.
loughneagheels.com

SCOTTISH HIGHLANDS
Wild Hearth Wood Fired Bakery
A wood-fired artisan bakery on the edge of the Scottish Highlands where everything is made using a sourdough starter.
wildhearthbakery.com
Strathearn Cheese Co.
A relatively new cheesemaking business, producing artisan cheeses with local milk and flavours, operating from the Cultybraggan camp (a WWII prisoner of war camp) in Perthshire.
strathearncheese.co.uk
Jamie Hammond at Cassafuir Farm, Stirlingshire
Jamie and wife Natalie farm and supply Scottish red deer for venison to Dovecote Park, Yorkshire. Jamie also has a role as a wildlife management officer for Scottish National Heritage.
Mountain Café, Aviemore
Providing award-winning food by a Kiwi chef, with an amazing view of the Cairngorm Mountains.
mountaincafe-aviemore.co.uk
Rothiemurchus
An estate at the forefront of wildlife and cultural conservation. Rothiemurchus cattle are traditionally reared, expertly butchered, and 'hung' on-site for four to six weeks. Their home-grown produce also includes venison, rainbow trout and heather honey.
rothiemurchus.net

ISLE OF SKYE
Mrs Mack's Farm Shop
A tiny farm shop in a shipping container positioned in the back garden of Mrs Mack's family farm in Torrin. She and her husband produce their own beef on the croft and sell it, along with coffee, cake and ice cream, from their little shop.
Facebook @MrsMacksFarmShop
Isle of Skye Baking Co.
Husband and wife team making 12 flavours of shortbread and eight of oatcakes, as well as other bakes, tablet and preserves.
isleofskyebakingco.co.uk

SHETLAND
Transition Turriefield
Without the use of chemical fertilisers, pesticides and herbicides, Penny and Allan grow most vegetables, such as salad, herbs, spring onions, chard, spinach and cauliflower in Transition Turriefield, on the very edge of mainland Shetland.
turriefieldveg.co.uk
Thule Ventus
A family business producing award-winning, air-dried salt cod (bacalao), using only cod from MSC-accredited sustainable Shetland stocks.
saltcod.co.uk

With thanks to all the chefs featured on the show:

Paul Ainsworth at No6, Padstow, Cornwall
Frances Atkins, The Yorke Arms, Harrogate, North Yorkshire
Kenny Atkinson, House of Tides, Newcastle, Tyne and Wear
Galton Blackiston, Morston Hall, Holt, Norfolk
Raymond Blanc, Le Manoir aux Quat'Saisons, Oxfordshire
Akshay Borges, The String, Shetland
Tessa Bramley, The Old Vicarage, Sheffield, South Yorkshire
James Close, Raby Hunt, Darlington, County Durham
Monica Galetti, Mere, London
Lisa Goodwin-Allen, Northcote, Blackburn, Lancashire
Shaun Hill, The Walnut Tree Inn, Abergavenny, Wales
Simon Hulstone, The Elephant, Torquay, Devon
Mark Jordan at the Beach, Jersey
Jude Kereama, Kota Kai, Newlyn, Cornwall
Chris McGowan, Wine & Brine, County Armagh, Northern Ireland
Nick Nairn Cook School, Stirlingshire, Scotland
Paul Rankin
Tony Singh
Michael Smith, Loch Bay Restaurant, Isle of Skye
Clare Smyth, Core, London
Mark Tamburrini, Royal Scotsman
Stephen Terry, The Hardwick, Abergavenny, Wales
Brian Turner
Gareth Ward, Ynyshir, Machynlleth, Wales
Susan and Bryan Webb, Tydynn Llan, Denbighshire, Wales

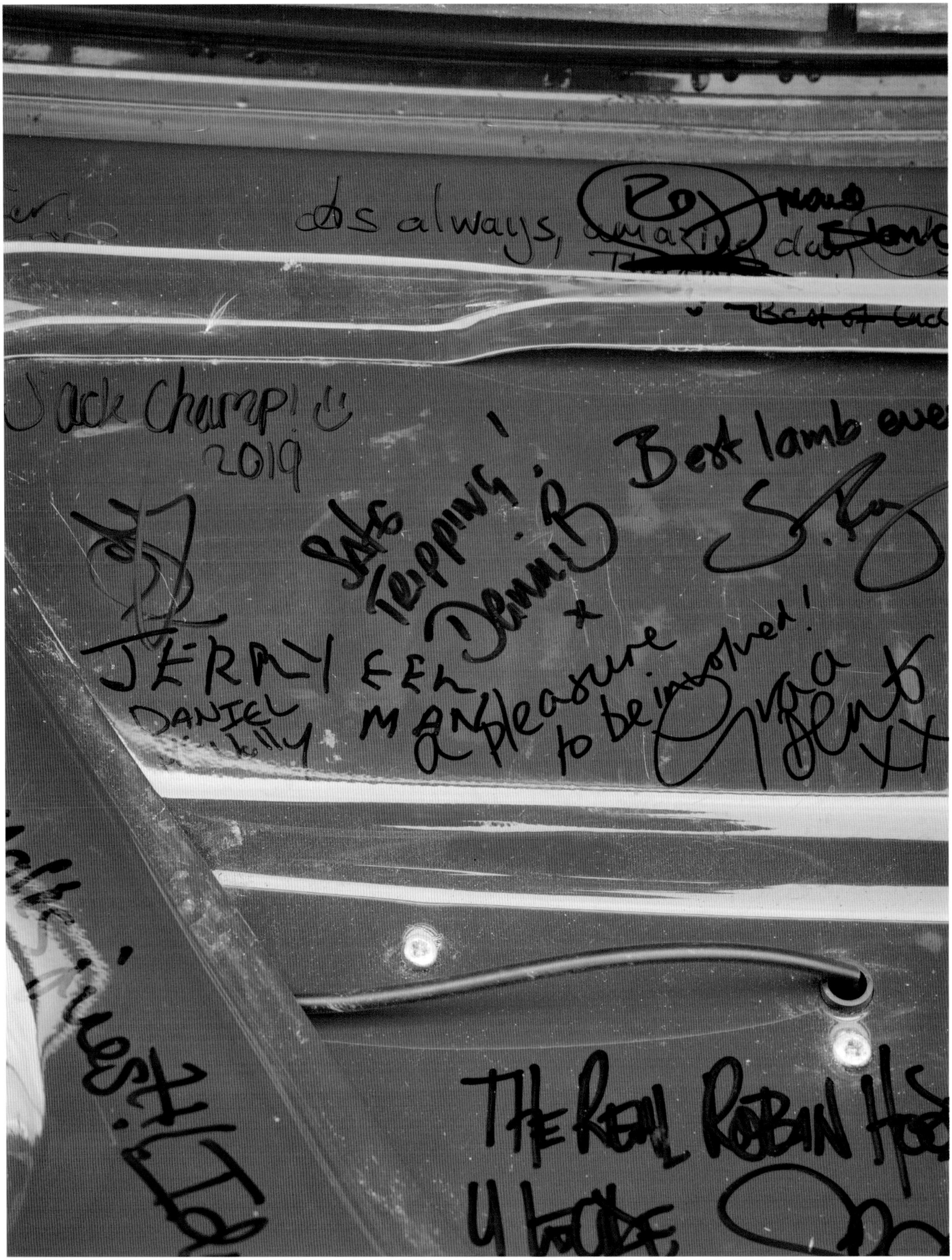

As always, amazing day Thanks

Ro

Best of luck

Jack Champ! ☺
2019

Safe Repping!
Dennis B

Best lamb ever

S. Roy

JERMY EEH
DANIEL
Kelly

a pleasure
to be involved!

X

Graha
Kent
XX

THE REAL ROBIN HOOD
U BOOKF,

ACKNOWLEDGEMENTS

A massive thank you to all of you that have helped make this series and book a reality. Sarah, Céline, Claire, Pete and all at Quadrille for masses of work putting this lot together and making sense of it – love working with you guys. Tom Kerridge for the foreword – huge thanks. Sam and all the food team involved in making the food and sorting out my spelling so that it makes some kind of sense. Vicky and Paul for being involved in making this show out of an idea in my head; Jonny, Ryan, James the mad dog and Ash for then making it look OK and sound OK on screen. Steve the young runner who managed to wreck only one car on the trip – thank god it wasn't mine. All the chefs and people who took part in this – without you all I wouldn't know where I'm going or what I'm doing and wouldn't enjoy it so much – so, for that, a massive massive thank you. And lastly Pippa, Fiona and Alison for filling the diary yet again and trying to manage the ever-growing jigsaw puzzle of days to make it all work.

LOVE TO YOU ALL, J

Publishing director: Sarah Lavelle
Senior commissioning editor: Céline Hughes
Project editor: Emily Preece-Morrison
Head of design: Claire Rochford
Junior designer: Alicia House
Photography: Peter Cassidy
Front cover photography: David Venni
Cover hair and make up: Alice Theobold
Cover fashion stylist: Rachel Gold
Food preparation and styling:
James Martin and Sam Head
Props stylist: Polly Webb-Wilson
Home economists: Sam Head and
Emma Marsden
Head of production: Stephen Lang
Production controller: Nikolaus Ginelli

First published in 2020 by Quadrille Publishing, an imprint of Hardie Grant Publishing
Quadrille, 52–54 Southwark Street,
London SE1 1UN
www.quadrille.com

Text © 2020 James Martin
Photography © 2020 Peter Cassidy
Design and layout © 2020 Quadrille Publishing

Cataloguing in Publication Data: a catalogue record for this book Is available from the British Library.

ISBN: 978 178713 525 3

Printed in China